MY GIRLFRIEND'S PREGNANT!

A TEEN'S GUIDE TO BECOMING A DAD

CHLOE SHANTZ-HILKES

annick press
toronto + new york + vancouver

Annick Press Ltd.

We acknowledge the support of the Canada Council for the Arts, the Ontario Arts Council, and the Government of Canada through the Canada Book Fund (CBF) for our publishing activities.

ONTARIO ARTS COUNCIL
CONSEIL DES ARTS DE L'ONTARIO
an Ontario government agency
un organisme du gouvernement de l'Ontario

Quotes included from *THE CURRENT – The Boy with the Past* – February 9, 2012 used with permission of CBC Licensing.

Cataloging in Publication
Shantz-Hilkes, Chloe, author
      My girlfriend's pregnant! / written by Chloe Shantz-Hilkes ; illustrated by Willow Dawson.

Issued in print and electronic formats.
ISBN 978-1-55451-742-8 (pbk.).–ISBN 978-1-55451-743-5 (bound).–
ISBN 978-1-55451-744-2 (html).–ISBN 978-1-55451-745-9 (pdf)

      1. Teenage fathers–Psychology. 2. Teenage fathers–Life skills guides.
3. Pregnancy–Psychological aspects. 4. Parenthood–Psychological aspects.
I. Title

HQ756.7.S53 2015   306.874'2   C2015-900841-7
                                                                 C2015-900842-5

Printed in Canada

MIX
Paper from
responsible sources
FSC® C004071

Visit us at: www.annickpress.com

Also available in e-book format. Please visit www.annickpress.com/ebooks.html for more details.
Or scan

CONTENTS

ACKNOWLEDGEMENTS

This book would not have been possible without the support and contributions of many people. First and foremost, my heartfelt thanks go out to each and every young dad who chose to share his experience of fatherhood with me. In some cases, reminiscing about pregnancy, abortion, childbirth, adoption, and/or parenting meant revisiting painful memories and times of regret. I am forever grateful to all the participating dads for their openness with me and with readers. I have no doubt that your stories will help other stressed out young fathers make tough choices and feel less alone along the way!

I am also grateful to Dr. Gary Clapton, Marlon Merrano, Mike White, Cheryl Dobinson, and the wonderful team at Annick Press for their contributions. As well, my thanks go out to the countless case workers, counselors, and medical professionals who provided me with vital information and access to young dads.

Thank you to the Ontario Arts Council for Writer's Reserve Grant that enabled me to complete this project.

Finally, thanks always to my family and my partner Chris for their continual support.

FOREWORD

I was in my last year of university when my girlfriend told me she was pregnant. My first thought was "No, not yet! I'm so close to finishing!" I had many examples of what to do and many opinions on how to do it, but I wasn't in a place where I could use any of what I saw or heard.

I was raised in a large family, the last of nine children. As an immigrant boy from Jamaica living in Toronto, I was surrounded by the good, the bad, and the ugly in life. My high school teachers probably figured I would be in jail by age 19; they certainly would not have seen me as father material. Some would say the chances were low that I would grow up to be a father of three amazing girls and have an excellent career. I'm glad to tell you they were wrong.

Have you ever felt very alone in a crowded room of family and friends? This is what being a father often felt like to me. I spent many years pretending I knew what I was doing, faking it until making it.

The great thing about life is that you are never prepared for it—it just happens. And as you will read throughout *My Girlfriend's Pregnant!* becoming a father can be just like that—sometimes it just happens. I had to learn the hard way, just by being a father.

Much later in life I had a second child who was planned, and I thought that would be so much easier. But having a second child was also really hard. And my third child? Yes, learning to be a father to her was hard too.

What really made a difference for me was to create a small community of people and friends that would encourage,

assist, and challenge me to be a better person and thus a better father. It also helped that I worked with other young men and women to share their stories in order to help themselves and other young people.

You will read similar stories in this book, and you will feel the young fathers' anger and excitement and hear the solutions that worked for them. You're not alone in this journey to fatherhood.

I used my earlier life challenges and experience to develop programs and services for children, youth, and newcomers in communities across the city of Toronto. Some of these have been services and programs geared to homeless youth, youth in the child welfare system, and youth who experience extreme poverty or violence. Having held leadership positions in several Toronto community agencies, I have seen many situations where young people are in despair. Many face challenges of poverty, some face challenges in just trying to fit in, and others are not supported by their families. One thing I have learned from the thousands of youth I have worked with or talked to is that these situations don't dictate how their future as fathers or mothers will turn out.

When I encounter youth I used to work with, I usually find out how well they are doing. The thing that changed for them and made the biggest difference was trusting a friend, a family member, or other adults. Working with young men and women, I have heard all the excuses in the world for why they will fail. When you're scared and feel ill prepared and unsupported, those excuses become a comfort to you. A better approach is to connect with the right person or information and use that to change your situation for the better. Working with youth has taught me to trust and support young people because they can succeed when given the right support, opportunity, and most of all love.

There are few places for young men to discuss their fears in general let alone their fears around fatherhood. If you're reading this book you are already one step ahead in becoming a great father. *My Girlfriend's Pregnant!* discusses the fears and gives you information and real stories, just like mine and yours. This book will not solve all of your problems, but it will help lead you to your own answers to questions about becoming a father.

Just remember that you are not alone. Being a father is never going to be easy—but it is always going to be amazing.

Marlon Merraro
Manager Urban Issues
Toronto Public Health

INTRODUCTION

Teenage pregnancy is something we hear a lot about. TV shows like *16 and Pregnant* and *Teen Mom* follow teenage parents before and after the births of their babies and give viewers a sense of what it's like to be young moms and dads. According to some research, shows like these have also helped lower teenage pregnancy rates, leading to increased contraception use in areas where more young viewers tuned in. But critics argue that these programs also glorify teenage pregnancy, making it seem more manageable than it really is. Politicians, meanwhile, treat teenage pregnancy as a problem that needs solving. And teenagers' parents—generally speaking—dread it.

Whether they're condemning young parents, applauding them, or trying to help them, most shows, articles, self-help books, and documentaries dealing with early parenthood focus on moms. When they're portrayed at all, young dads are frequently depicted as irresponsible and uninvolved. Research and social programs also tend to ignore young fathers. They're too often assumed to be uninterested in their kids, disrespectful toward their partners, and undeserving of support. All in all, young men who find themselves fathers can face a lot of stigma.

It's true that some young dads are deadbeats. But a lot of them aren't. Recently, a group of fathers in their teens and twenties sought to shed light on their realities by producing their *own* documentary called *Dads Matter Too*. In the film, they talk about the stress and challenges associated with fatherhood—but also the joys, and their efforts to play a role in their kids' lives.

> **WE ARE QUITE MISUNDERSTOOD. WE DO WANT TO LEARN. WE DO WANT GOOD THINGS. AND WE JUST DON'T WANT TO BE JUDGED WRONG BY ANYONE.**

***

> **ALL OF US DADS AIN'T JUST SELFISH SCREWUPS. SOME OF US ARE ACTUALLY WILLING AND THERE FOR OUR CHILDREN AND WANNA BE; EVEN THOUGH IN EVERY CIRCUMSTANCE IT'S NOT PERFECT AND [SOMETIMES] WE CAN'T BE, WE STILL WANT TO BE THERE FOR OUR CHILDREN.**

***

> **FATHERS ARE THERE TOO. AND THEY DO WANT TO BE INVOLVED.**

***

> **DADS ARE THERE AS WELL, AND WE ARE DOING—MOST DADS ARE ACTUALLY DOING THEIR PART.**

While writing this book, I interviewed many young men across the country. Some of them were single and some were in relationships. Some of them had many kids and some had partners who chose to have abortions. Some were brand new or expectant parents and others considered themselves veterans. Many of them said they wished they had used contraception and were scared to discover they were going to become fathers. All of them were honest about how hard dealing with a pregnancy can be. They talked about the difficulties of choosing—or watching their partners choose—between parenting, adoption, or abortion. They talked about the stress of sleepless nights, diapers, and day care. In many cases, they talked about regret or wishing things had gone differently. But their stories are also a testament to the fact that being a young dad has its ups as well as its downs. Above all, these young fathers are keen to challenge the assumptions people make about them. And, perhaps most importantly, their stories offer insights to other young men whose lives may be affected by a pregnancy—planned or unplanned. My hope is that this book will therefore help readers understand three things:

- Young dads are not alone.
- Young dads always have options.
- Young dads don't need to accept the assumptions and judgments people make.

HOW TO READ THIS BOOK

This is one of very few resources on pregnancy and parenthood geared specifically toward *young men*. But for the hundreds of thousands of teenage girls who become pregnant each year in North America and around the world, there are hundreds of thousands of dads in their teens and twenties. In some cases, these young men may never even find out about their partners' pregnancies. And in others, young women may decide to terminate unplanned pregnancies (see Chapter Six for more information on abortion). But no matter the outcome of a pregnancy, knowing about it is sure to have an effect on young fathers. This book explores what it is like to discover that your partner is pregnant; the effects of abortion, adoption, and childbirth on young fathers; the experience of parenthood itself; where to turn for help and support; how parenthood can affect relationships; and much, much more.

You may be reading this book because
- you or someone you know is a young dad or is about to become one
- you're worried or wondering about the *possibility* of becoming a young dad
- your partner is currently deciding how to deal with an unplanned pregnancy
- someone in your life asked you to read it

● you're simply curious about the experiences of young
fathers

Whatever your reasons for picking up a copy of this book,
there is no right or wrong way to read it. You may decide to
go from cover to cover, or to pick and choose from sections
that intrigue you. If there's a particular issue you're most inter-
ested in, take a look at the index at the very back of the book
and find the pages that deal with that topic.

However you choose to read this book, know that it may
leave you with more questions than answers. That's largely
because there is no "right" way to approach young fatherhood
or respond to the news of an unplanned pregnancy. Hopefully
the true stories of the young fathers who took part in this
project will help you figure out what decisions might be right
for you. Also be sure to check out the Further Resources section at the back of this book for a list of other great resources
on being a young dad.

Chapter One

FINDING OUT

Young dads share their experiences of discovering their partners were pregnant and talk about how they decided what to do next

A vast majority of early pregnancies are unplanned. According to most research, about four out of five teenage pregnancies come as a surprise to the young men and women involved. Often, this is because contraception wasn't used. Sometimes, however, the incorrect use of contraception is to blame. In fact, one recent study found that nearly half of unintended pregnancies happened despite the use of some form of birth control! Statistics like these are a reminder of just how important it is for young men and women alike to fully understand how their chosen forms of birth control really work, and what could make them more or less effective.

The pill (used by more than 12 million women in the United States) is effective 99.7 percent of the time if used properly. But if the user misses a pill—or even takes one late—the drug's effectiveness decreases. Other popular methods of contraception (pulling out, for example) are far less reliable, failing to prevent pregnancy up to 18 percent of the time. (And, keep in mind, neither the pill nor pulling out protects from sexually transmitted infections!) It's important for sexually active partners hoping to avoid unplanned pregnancy to be honest with each other about what forms of protection they're using, and to ask their health care providers or other trusted adults if they have questions about these methods.

»TRUE/FALSE«
PULLING OUT PREVENTS AGAINST SEXUALLY TRANSMITTED INFECTIONS.

You may encounter a *lot* of different health care workers during a pregnancy, whether it's planned or unplanned.

Your *GP* (a.k.a. "general practitioner") is a doctor who doesn't have a particular specialty. They're an all-around medical expert, and the person you and your partner should consult with regularly about any health-related issues—pregnancy or otherwise.

Midwives are certified medical professionals who can deliver babies in many home and healthcare settings, depending on the jurisdiction. They generally promote alternatives to the routine use of drugs during pregnancy and childbirth, and emphasize holistic pre- and post-birth care.

A *doula* is sometimes referred to as a "labor coach." Doulas are not *technically* medical professionals and are not qualified to deliver babies on their own. Instead, they assist women and their partners before, during, and after childbirth by providing physical and emotional support. Most insurance companies will not cover the cost of hiring a doula, and the doula industry is not regulated.

OB-GYN is an abbreviation for *obstetrics-gynecology*. Obstetrics specialists deal with pregnancy and childbirth specifically. Gynecology specialists deal with women's reproductive health more broadly. All certified OB-GYNs are doctors who have completed these specializations in addition to a standard medical degree. Not every woman sees an OB-GYN when she is pregnant, but many GPs refer women to one.

You may also encounter *social workers* during your partner's pregnancy. In most countries social workers are licensed, and the social work industry is regulated. Social workers can connect you and your partner with various agencies that might be able to help you find employment, accommodation, and access to the other kinds of care listed here.

Even perfect use of a reliable form of birth control can sometimes fail to prevent pregnancy. That's part of the reason that, despite recent declines in teenage pregnancy rates, hundreds of thousands of babies are still born to teenage parents in North America each year. If you're a young dad—or soon to become one—that means you're not alone. Unfortunately, that probably doesn't make finding out about an unplanned pregnancy any less of a shock.

> I was only 15 when she came to me and said, "Shane, what if I was pregnant?" I thought it was a hypothetical question at first. Once we knew for sure, we were both so scared. I just remember this huge sense of anxiety. —*Shane*

> I was away at college when I found out. I came home for a visit one weekend, and my girlfriend Maria told me on the way home from the bus stop. We'd been using protection, so it was such a shock. Plus it turned out she was already six months along, and so it was too late for an abortion or anything. It was like hitting a brick wall. —*Jason*

My girlfriend told me on a phone call because
we were dating long-distance at the time. It
was an enormous shock, but I wasn't really
scared or anything. I think I assumed right away
that she would get an abortion. — *Geoff*

I didn't believe it at first. I thought she was
trying to trick me (she'd tried before). Once the
proof of that was in front of me I remember
feeling sad about the life I was being asked to
give up, but also happy about the possibility of
becoming a dad. I'll tell you one thing though: I
definitely wasn't ready. — *Dylan*

Research says young men whose partners' pregnancies were
unplanned continue to feel more stress during gestation
and in the early days of parenting than the dads of "planned"
babies. In other words, that initial sense of shock can take a
long time to wear off.

When I first met my girlfriend, her doctor had
told her that she had a lump on her cervix that
would prevent her from ever having kids. But
then one day she missed her period. And then

we found out she was pregnant. I remember being scared and confused. This wasn't supposed to have happened! Even now, seven months after we found out—with our daughter about to arrive—I feel nervous a lot. Sometimes I don't know if I'll be able to do this. —*Graeme*

Things don't always go as planned, and emergency contraceptives such as "Plan B" or "ella" can be used to prevent pregnancy in the event that a couple's ordinary birth control method fails (e.g., the condom breaks). These drugs can be used by a woman up to five days after unprotected sex, but are most effective if used in the first twenty-four hours. Remember, emergency contraceptives prevent pregnancy and are not a form of abortion. If you and your partner have had unprotected sex and want to prevent pregnancy, encourage her to speak with a pharmacist about emergency contraception.

»TRUE/FALSE «
EMERGENCY CONTRACEPTIVES ARE A FORM OF ABORTION.

Later chapters of this book talk at length about deciding how to deal with an unplanned pregnancy. For now, here are a few important things to start considering as soon as you find out you might be having a child:

- **HOW WILL YOUR LIFE CHANGE IF YOU HAVE A BABY?** Your life will change dramatically if you become a father. Think carefully about what these changes might be. How will your social life be affected? How will your plans for the future have to evolve? Will you be able to finish high school—or college—on schedule? Will you be able to keep your job, if you have one? It's important that you prepare for these changes, and don't let them catch you off guard.

- **IS THIS WHAT YOU WANT?** Other people are bound to have opinions about what you and your partner should do. They may be very forceful about these opinions, pressuring you to keep the baby— or give it up. Ultimately, decisions about a woman's body are hers alone. You'll have decisions to make too, however.

- **CAN YOU AFFORD IT?** According to most estimates, raising a child until they're eighteen can cost well over $200,000. And many of those costs come up front in the form of car seats, strollers, cribs, diapers, and playpens. Some sources of financial support are available to young parents, but it's important you and your partner are honest with yourselves about whether parenthood is something you'll be able to pay for.

> I hate putting it this way, but in a way my
> life would have been over if I had become a
> full-time parent at that age. I had so many
> ambitions. Above all, I wanted to finish my
> degree, and I probably wouldn't have been able
> to do that with a kid. —*Jason*

The questions don't stop here. Through all the ups and downs of finding out about an unintended pregnancy, one of the hardest parts for many young dads is deciding when and how to tell their own parents: the soon-to-be grandparents. After all, while many are supportive, some are not.

> My parents were pretty pissed ... my mom
> especially. I remember her saying, "How could
> you do this to me, Shane?!" She was more
> worried about the fact that she was too young
> to have grandkids than she was about the fact
> that I was too young to be a dad! —*Shane*

> I actually met my girlfriend when she was
> already a month pregnant with another guy's kid.
> I found out after we'd been dating a few weeks,
> and I decided to stick around. I vividly remember
> telling my parents. My life had gone totally off
> the rails in their opinion. They basically wrote me
> off and kicked me out of the house. —*Steve*

***

My girlfriend's mom took it the worst. She was really mad and said she didn't want me coming by the house anymore, but she eventually got over that. My parents weren't too impressed either, but nobody ever suggested we should give Luke up for adoption or that Catherine

should have an abortion. Eventually, everyone realized that we were having this baby and the best thing they could do was to support us.
— *Patrick*

Telling your parents (or your partner's parents) about an unplanned pregnancy can be daunting, to say the least. Unfortunately, there's no road map for breaking the news. But most of the young dads I spoke with said things got easier every day after the first conversation. Many of their parents who were disappointed or downright livid at first gradually became supportive. In other words, telling your parents you got a girl pregnant can be a bit like ripping off a bandage: it might hurt like hell, but you're usually better off getting it over with.

At first, I was more afraid of my mother's reaction than I was of the outcome of the pregnancy. I eventually grabbed a piece of paper from the notepad by the phone and I just wrote: *My girlfriend is pregnant.* Then I folded it up, put it in her lunch bag, said goodbye, and left for school. – *Chris* (interviewed by CBC Radio's Aziza Sindhu in *The Boy with the Past*)

While most teen pregnancies are unplanned, some are not. In fact, about 15 percent of teenage pregnancies are planned. Sure enough, this was the case for a number of the young men I spoke with. They told me that even though everyone tends to assume their kids were a surprise, they weren't at all.

»TRUE/FALSE«
MANY TEENAGE COUPLES ACTUALLY INTEND TO GET PREGNANT.

I'd always wanted a son, and I knew from the moment the doctor said, "You guys are pregnant," that it was a boy and I was going to name him after my dad. It was a really exciting moment for me. I believe my first words outside of the clinic were me shouting at the top of my lungs, "I'm going to be a dad!" I was exuberantly excited. —*Daniel*

Even if a pregnancy was planned or comes as welcome news, however, coping with the anxiety that comes with finding out you're going to be a dad is often no easy task.

> When my girlfriend and I were in our late teens, we just kind of had the urge to have a kid. So we went for it. The first time she got pregnant she had a miscarriage, but after that everything happened so quickly. I remember being a bit surprised that it was so easy after that first try. Suddenly it was like: *Oh man ... This is happening!* I'm not going to say it was a mistake, but things moved very, very fast.
> — *Kale*

> I was 19 and Jaimie was 17, and we basically wanted to have a kid. We weren't *trying,* necessarily, but we'd talked about it, and when we found we were pretty happy. It wasn't until Luke was born that I realized I had no idea what I was doing. Once the initial excitement wore off a bit I started thinking: *Crap ... What did I just do?* — *Matt*

The kind of anxiety described by all of these young dads is a perfectly normal response to the stress associated with finding out you're going to be a parent. Heck, first-time parents in their thirties and forties will tell you that they too experienced many of these same emotions upon finding out they were going to have a baby.

In some cases, anxiety can be a good thing. If you're worried about passing a test or nailing a job interview, it can help you focus and give you a boost of adrenaline to help you overcome your nerves. Experiencing anxiety over a sustained period of time or to an extreme degree, however, can negatively affect your body, your relationships, and your ability to prepare for parenthood. If you're feeling anxious, try to find someone to talk to. This could be a therapist, social worker— or just a friend you really trust. In more extreme cases, you may want to consider seeking professional, medical help. For more on coping with the anxiety and stress associated with young parenthood, check out Chapter Eight.

Cognitive behavioral therapy is a form of talk therapy that is commonly used by people of all ages to help manage a wide range of problems, including anxiety. Usually, CBT involves face-to-face sessions with a trained therapist. These sessions are designed to help patients understand that, while they can't always control their circumstances, they can control the ways they respond to them. This realization was important for a lot of the young dads I spoke with, whether they got to it through therapy or on their own.

Relaxation techniques, cognitive behavioral therapy, and medication prescribed by a psychiatrist can all help with anxiety

management. In some cases, simple changes like ensuring you get enough sleep, exercise, and healthy food can also make a huge difference. But step one is often finding someone to confide in—or knowing when it's time to ask for help.

Sometimes I'll talk to my girlfriend and she'll tell me to write or draw or do something to take my mind off of everything. It's a good way to unwind. And sometimes I'll call my grandma. She usually tells me to take it day by day. That sounds simple, I know, but it helps. I also have a social worker that I talk to sometimes. He's a really active guy, so whenever we meet up he'll have some activity planned for us. —*Graeme*

Whatever you do, remember that the anxiety you may be feeling because of a partner's pregnancy is *completely normal*. As obvious as it may sound, accepting that your feelings are normal is usually a step in the direction of coping and of moving forward with the decisions you now have to make.

Chapter Two

PREGNANCY AND CHILDBIRTH

Young dads talk about their partners' pregnancies and their babies' births

A woman's pregnancy usually lasts about thirty-eight weeks from the day of conception. Weeks 1–13 are referred to as the first trimester; weeks 13–28 are the second; and weeks 29–birth are the third. Most fetuses become "viable" (capable of surviving outside the womb) early in the third trimester. The safest births, however, usually occur between weeks 37 and 41.

> *Embryo* is the term used up until the eighth week of a woman's pregnancy. After this, the term *fetus* is used up until the birth.

Pregnancy is a natural and normal occurrence, and the human body is—generally speaking—built for it. With good medical care, most women find pregnancy to be a largely positive experience. In some cases, however, things can go wrong. And teen pregnancies are especially prone to complications. In particular, teen moms are more likely to experience soreness of the breasts and vaginal bleeding during their pregnancies. And the babies of teenage mothers are more likely to be born prematurely. What's more, even the healthiest of pregnancies can include nausea, vomiting, fatigue, and other symptoms.

»TRUE/FALSE«

IN RARE CASES, WOMEN (ESPECIALLY YOUNG WOMEN) MAY EXPERIENCE VAGINAL BLEEDING DURING PREGNANCY.

This is not the same thing as menstruation, but it could theoretically be hard to tell the difference, especially if the woman is used to having irregular periods. Although it may be nothing, vaginal bleeding during pregnancy can be a sign of trouble. If your partner is experiencing vaginal bleeding during pregnancy, she should talk to her doctor right away.

For the most part, young dads should not be alarmed if their partners experience these sorts of things. Some symptoms (including leg cramps, frequent dizziness, or severe abdominal pains) can be cause for concern, however. A good rule is to make sure you and your partner are in regular contact with a medical professional you trust (an OB-GYN, GP, or midwife) during her pregnancy. This person will advise your partner on prenatal nutrition, exercise, sleep, and more. If either of you ever feels nervous about something she's experiencing, call them.

Ask whether what you're experiencing is normal. Chances are you'll be reassured. If not, you'll get the help you need.

> Unfortunately, Laura was put on bed rest for part of her pregnancy because she had a rare condition where there was too much amniotic fluid in her uterus. I loved taking care of her, though. She wasn't supposed to get up and cook for herself or anything. So I would cook dinners and get the groceries and look after her. I sang to her belly every day. — *Daniel*

> While Catherine was pregnant for the first time, I didn't have a good job and so our income wasn't great. Our relationships with our families weren't very good either. I was living with my sister in a one-bedroom apartment, and Catherine was like an hour away living with her family. Basically, there were a lot of things about our circumstances that could have been better. We were excited but also very, very stressed. — *Patrick*

Even with months to prepare, many of the young dads I spoke with said their babies were born before they knew it.

Fortunately—and perhaps unlike their girlfriends—most of them described childbirth itself as a positive experience.

> When Gemma arrived I was one of those dads who watched the whole thing, wide-eyed. I was like, *this is unbelievable*. I've met some other young dads through support groups and stuff who say they found childbirth really gross, but to me it was too amazing to miss. It's a very strange feeling when you hold your kid for the first time. Everything that's happened before that suddenly seems less important. Your life becomes about them ... connected to theirs.
> —*Steve*

> The day Michael was born I was ecstatic. I was absolutely ecstatic. I still remember the moment I got to hold him for the first time. That rush is absolutely, inexplicably amazing. And it was that rush that told me: this is gonna be worth it. —*Shane*

> By the time we were in the hospital waiting for Luke to arrive I didn't care about any of the drama anymore. I just couldn't wait to meet him. By then our families had finally come

around and were giving us a lot more support. It's weird because before I started dating Catherine I actually didn't think I ever wanted kids. But as soon as Luke was born I felt like going back in time to punch my old self in the face. I suddenly couldn't imagine not having my kid. — *Patrick*

If you have trained health-care professionals at your side, childbirth is almost always very safe. Sadly, a vast majority of the complications that occur in childbirth are preventable, and happen in parts of the world that don't have widespread access to modern medicine. Things can still go wrong even in the best of circumstances, however. Preterm births, in particular, are prone to complications. If your baby's birth doesn't go according to plan, the fear and even panic you're likely to feel are completely understandable.

The birth itself was really scary. Right after Britney was born, she was rushed to the Children's Hospital. She was a really, really big baby (13 pounds [5.9 kg]!), and they had to put her on a machine to help her breathe. She spent two weeks in the ICU. I remember it was kind of weird because where they had her she was surrounded by premature babies who were all like 5 pounds or less. She looked *huge*. — *Matt*

***

When Brian was born he wasn't breathing. His lungs had filled up with amniotic fluid from Laura giving birth, and so the doctors had to suction out his lungs. Then we found out that he had something called a ventricular septal defect (which was basically a hole in his heart). So the doctors told us there was a 60 percent chance that he would need open-heart surgery before he was six months old. He beat those odds, but it was a lot to deal with. It still is.
—*Daniel*

***

We were at the hospital for hours. We would both kind of drift off, and then another contraction would come and Maria would squeeze my hand. She was supposed to get some drugs to help her through the pain, but we were alone in the room for so long that by the time the nurse came back it was too late for that, and she had to give birth without them. —*Jason*

The good news is that scary birth stories are rare. That's one reason to consider joining a support group for young moms and dads. Hearing about other people's experiences of childbirth may help you feel more at ease with

what you're about to go through. Dads in these groups may spend their time learning how to serve as birth coaches, helping their partners through labor; practicing infant CPR and first aid; or simply playing sports, making music, and doing other activities *unrelated* to parenting.

> Do the maternity classes. Those are really
> helpful. It's so good to be around other people
> going through the same stuff as you at the
> same time as you. —*Matt*

> The first course I took—called *Infant Simulation*—
> was kind of a gateway class for me. I got sort
> of hooked on them after that. Another course
> (called It's My Child Too) was just for fathers,
> and it taught me all about what to expect and
> how to make sure that my daughter would feel
> comfortable with me. —*Dylan*

The bottom line is that in industrialized countries, pregnancy and childbirth are very safe. In fact, in the United States and Canada, the maternal mortality rate is less than 0.02 percent! Still, if you're feeling anxious about your partner's pregnancy or your baby's birth, be sure to consult some of the resources listed in the Further Resources section. Part of what tends to make us anxious can be fear of the unknown—so get to know pregnancy and childbirth!

Chapter Three

PARENTING

From the delivery room to diapers and daycare

Like it or not, there are a *lot* of statistics out there that confirm what so many of the young dads I spoke with had to say: life as a young parent is not easy. According to Planned Parenthood in the United States, teenage parents

- are more likely to be poor
- are less likely to finish high school
- are less likely to go to college
- are more likely to face health-related problems (e.g., addiction and depression)

This is a bit of a chicken-and-egg scenario. On the one hand, becoming a parent at an early age can increase your risk of all these things. Staying in school and finding steady work is hard when you're busy being a dad! On the other hand, many of these factors also increase your risk of becoming a parent in the first place. Statistics show that low-income teenagers are consistently the most likely to experience unplanned pregnancy.

> My dad was just eighteen when he had me and only seventeen when he had my sister. There was definitely a lot less stability when we were kids because of how young he was. I think he

really wanted to create a world where everyone was safe and provided for, but there was just too much uncertainty. When I compare my dad's situation to my life (I got married, then bought a house, then had a baby) I feel so relieved. We're not trying to juggle. Everything isn't up in the air. — *Ethan*

Of course, there are exceptions to all of these rules. Some young parents come from privileged families. Many go on to finish school and have successful professional lives. But however you slice it, young parents have the deck stacked against them in all kinds of ways.

This is one of many reasons that young couples who face an unplanned pregnancy may choose to terminate the pregnancy, or release the baby for adoption. Chapters Six and Seven in this book talk about the experiences of young men whose stories involve abortion or adoption rather than parenting. Some of them regret these decisions, but others are comfortable with the way things turned out, and happy to have avoided the stress and hardship associated with being a young dad. Of course, this does not mean that young parenting is always a bad experience. For every dad I spoke with who chose to become a parent, there have been good days and bad. In many cases, the bad days began with sleepless nights.

There were a lot of sleepless nights — especially when she first got home from the hospital. Back then, I had to do most of the childcare because Sandra had a caesarean section and it took her a while to recover. So I would literally be up all night, and I started having horrible headaches. A few weeks into this, I actually ended up in the hospital myself because of stress. After that, I learned that if I was totally exhausted, I wasn't going to be able to help anyone. —*Matt*

A *caesarean section* is a type of surgery used to deliver babies when a vaginal birth would put the baby or mother at risk. It involves making an incision in the mother's abdomen through which the baby is removed. Although fairly common, caesarean sections (also known as "c-sections") do increase the level of risk associated with childbirth and are best avoided unless medically necessary.

I'm one of those guys who read all the prenatal books: how to prepare myself, prepare the house, prepare everything. So I thought I was prepared, but actually becoming a dad taught me so much more than any book could. One of the things I was least prepared for was sleep deprivation. I can't tell you how many times I put Gemma in her stroller and walked her around the block, watching the sun come up, knowing I had to be at work in a few hours. And when you're running on three hours of sleep day after day, you start having these really strange thoughts that don't make any sense. —*Steve*

Those first few months after Luke was born were pretty stressful. I moved back in with my parents to save money, and Catherine and Luke stayed with her mom. That meant we were living like five hours apart at first. I would do my best to see them as much as I could, but it meant I was always on the road really late at night, getting hardly any sleep. This went on for about two years, and it was really hard on all of us. —*Patrick*

Believe it or not, most newborn babies actually sleep *a lot*, just never for many hours at a time. This is because their tiny

stomachs can't hold much food, meaning they need to be fed every few
hours around the clock. Most parents
of newborns are lucky to get three
or four hours of uninterrupted sleep
a night.

Sustained sleeplessness can have
all kinds of consequences, ranging
from irritability and depression to achy
muscles, headaches, and weight gain.
Of course, *some* sleep deprivation is a
normal part of being a new parent, but
it's important to try to make sure you
and your partner get as much sleep as possible. This might
involve taking turns feeding your baby at night or rearrang-
ing your schedules to allow for daytime naps. Maybe it means
asking grandma or grandpa to be on baby duty one night. As
Matt puts it, you're no help to anyone if you're completely
exhausted all the time.

When you think about it, sleepless nights are something all
parents face regardless of their age. But for young parents, these
everyday challenges are combined with extraordinary ones, like
missing out on the normalcy of your teens and twenties.

I sometimes feel like I live my life under a rock.
I mean, I have family members and friends and
stuff who will sometimes babysit so I can have
a night off or whatever. But now that I'm a
dad I never go to the movies or go out. I don't
know anything about pop culture or the stuff

other people talk about. Kids' shows are on 24/7 at my house, so I hardly ever get to watch the news. I never know what's going on in the world. I don't even have e-mail! —*Kale*

It was really hard to have a kid way before any of my friends. We'd be invited to New Year's and Halloween parties, and we'd have to say no, no, no. —*Steve*

A couple of years after Luke was born, Catherine found out she was pregnant again. I remember feeling like *what the heck am I going to do?* I was only twenty and already had one kid I couldn't really provide for. Now here was another one?! I started partying, going out drinking, and spending money on things I couldn't afford. I eventually got over that, but it meant I had to give up being able to do whatever I wanted whenever I wanted. We have to schedule everything around the kids now, and my whole life feels like a calendar. —*Patrick*

For young parents, balancing work and/or school can be extremely difficult. Some young dads and moms are lucky enough to have the support of relatives. But if they don't, being a young parent can mean looking for the kind of work you wouldn't ordinarily be seeking for years to come. After all, baby paraphernalia can cost a lot!

I think the biggest challenge for Evelyn and me was that we weren't in a great financial situation. I guess that's why a lot of people wait until their thirties to have kids. For us, money was tight, and there were a lot of times I had to borrow from my mom to get baby formula and diapers. — *Steve*

I don't think there's any golden, perfect age to become a dad. But I do think it's important to get to a point where you're truly independent — emotionally *and* financially. Maybe that's just my experience, but that was so important to me. You need your circle of friends to be supportive and your bank account to be decently full and all that. I guess in that sense, it's not age so much as circumstance that really matters. — *Ethan*

***

Alisha and I were able to manage the first two months after Michael was born thanks to the generosity of her sister and some close family friends. But after that I knew it was time for me to go get a job. At sixteen that's a pretty scary thing to do, though. Like normally this would be some part-time job to help save for university. But I was looking for something full-time that would pay enough for rent and baby formula and diapers! — *Shane*

Fortunately, there are lots of services in place to help young dads find work and access other forms of financial support. (See the Further Resources section.) The easiest way to take advantage of these resources is usually with the help of a community support worker. It can be difficult to navigate and apply for all the various programs you might have access to without their help. But with help, having a baby in your teens or early twenties doesn't have to mean choosing between work and school the way Shane did.

I was in grade 10 when we had Michael, and the only thing that made sense at the time was for me to quit school. That really sucked. A year and a half after he was born, I was able to go back to high school part-time and get through grades 10 and 11. I never did manage to graduate though. It was just too much. — *Shane*

» TRUE/FALSE «
IF YOU DROP OUT OF HIGH SCHOOL THERE IS NO WAY FOR YOU TO GO TO COLLEGE/UNIVERSITY.

The *General Educational Development test* (also known as the GED) is a test that gives students who did not finish high school the opportunity to get an equivalent diploma. The GED began as a way for young members of the military returning from World War II to earn their high school diplomas. In some places, learners must now be over the age of seventeen to take the GED tests, but there is no maximum age at which they can do so. Most regions also offer GED preparation courses to adult learners pursuing their high school diplomas. A student who fails the GED can almost always try again after a waiting period.

Being a young dad isn't all sleepless nights and compromises though. Far from it! Parenthood can also be filled with joy. And for some of the young dads I spoke with, becoming a father meant finding ways to turn the corner on lives that hadn't been going the way they'd planned.

Krista had our son Kieran while I was in prison. I spoke to my son for the first time on a telephone from behind one-inch-thick glass. When I finally got out, I managed to stop hanging out with the people who had me living so rough before jail. I suddenly had no trouble telling them to fuck off and leave me alone. Basically, I turned my life completely around because of my son. — *Kale*

***

Doing whatever I wanted was fun, but life feels more important now—more meaningful. I get to sit back and evaluate my priorities and figure out what really matters to me. And I never have to feel pressured to go somewhere or do something I don't want to because I can always say, "Sorry. I'm with my boys tonight." — *Patrick*

***

My dad drank every day, and that wasn't how I wanted to raise my boys. The big highlight for me is knowing that both my sons will have a responsible father. I think I am a pretty good father today now. I'm very aware of the fact that I'm making an impression. My whole way of life has really changed since becoming a parent, and it's changed for the better. — *Daniel*

***

I used to not care about anything ... drink,
smoke weed every day, cigarettes, not
care about what's in my body ... That's the
personality I had before I found out I was going
to have a child. As soon as Claire was born,
none of that mattered anymore. —*Dylan*

Many of these young dads admitted that they sometimes wish
they'd waited before having kids, but they were also quick to
highlight the benefits of parenthood. In particular, many of
them pointed out that whereas older parents sometimes have
a hard time keeping up with their growing, active kids, that
doesn't apply to them!

Being young makes being a dad hard, but it has
its upside too. I'm fit. I can keep up. By the time
Conner's ten, I'll still have plenty of energy to go
outside and kick a ball around with him without
my back killing me or whatever. —*Steve*

***

I think the fact that I'm a young dad has allowed me to bond more closely with my son. I'm not going to be one of those fathers that's like fifty when my son is fifteen. I'll still be young myself. I'll be able to throw a basketball around with him; I'll be able to keep up with him. —*Daniel*

From being able to keep up to being able to turn over a new leaf, fatherhood can be a positive force in many young dads' lives. But it's rarely easy. Money problems, sleep-lessness, and stress inevitably take their toll. If you've ever heard the old saying "Sleep, social life, and grades: pick two," you can probably imagine what adding kids to the equation does. You can read more about how to find balance in Chapter Eight, but in the meantime, here are some words of wisdom from two of the dads I spoke with:

I remember one day Ashley was sick and had a fever, so we took all her clothes off and she ended up pooping all over my ex. I wasn't laughing at the time, but I do now when I think about it. I guess I would say that in the end, all those rough periods only make you learn to appreciate the good times more. —*Matt*

***

You need to have patience. The answers of
parenting don't always come when you want
them to. You may need to take some time. With
time, I've become more and more confident as a
father. And I've learned not to worry about what
I can't see. Instead I worry about the here and
now—making it count. —*Shane*

Chapter Four

FATHER FROM AFAR

Young dads share their stories of separation and talk about how to find your way back to your kids

O ne of the stereotypes you hear most about young dads is that they tend to take off on their kids. In reality, however, there's not much statistical evidence to support the claim that young fathers are any more likely than older dads to be absent from their children's lives.

> People really respect me as a parent. They all tell me, "Oh man, you're so good. You've done so much for Claire. You're an amazing dad." And I think to myself, *I'm not doing anything special. I'm doing what everyone should do for their kids.* —Dylan

To be sure, young moms are still *much* more likely to play an active role in parenting, but research has found that over half of teen fathers participate in feeding, dressing, or playing with their child at least once a week, and provide financial support to their partners at least once a month.

> *Child support* is a term that refers to payments
> one parent makes to the other in the event of
> a separation. These payments are intended to
> pay for the needs of their child. Despite some
> recent increases in the number of single-*father*
> homes, the vast majority of child support is
> still paid by dads and is required by law. The
> amount to be paid is determined based on the
> father's income and a number of other factors,
> including local laws. In most cases, fathers
> who are single parenting are *also* entitled to
> child support payments from the mothers.

It's true that about one in three kids in the United States grows up in a home without their biological father. Many of these kids may still grow up in a home with multiple caregivers (whether that's two moms, two dads, grandparents, adoptive parents, stepparents, or something else entirely), but those who don't face a higher risk of being incarcerated, becoming teen parents themselves, and more. This means that a lot of teen dads are themselves more likely to have grown up without a father. But it's *also* true that dads who make an effort to be in their kids' lives can have a positive impact, even if they don't live with their children or have limited contact.

Many young dads who are separated from their children don't want to be. Chances are, they have varied and complicated reasons for being apart from their kids. In Matt's case, a messy breakup with Britney's mom prevents him from seeing his daughter. But if it were up to him, he would be in her life every day.

A lot of what happened had to do with the fact that I was kind of immature at the time. I did a lot of yelling and screaming and saying stupid things. I know now that I should've asked permission to come over and see Britney. I should have done things differently. I just want her to know that even though I'm not in her life I think about her all the time, and my door is always open to her. —Matt

For many young dads, walking away from a relationship can mean saying goodbye to their child too—at least temporarily. But let's face it: the relationships we're in in our teens and early twenties aren't necessarily ones we should be in forever. The next chapter deals more with young dads' relationships with their partners, but for now, it's important to acknowledge that sometimes young parents might need a little distance, even if that means distance from their kids.

After Sophia was born, her mom and I fought all the time. Erica was drinking a lot, and I would come home late to find her hammered and Sophia crying. Eventually things really blew up between us. After about a year of on-again-off-again

nonsense, I finally decided to get out of town. I knew that leaving my relationship with Erica meant leaving Sophia too. It killed me, but I did it. It had to be done. *—Martin*

The good news is that being separated from your child doesn't have to be permanent. Some of the dads I spoke to went from having zero contact with their kids to seeing them regularly. Others had to deal with situations so complicated that the courts intervened. In Martin's case, a judge even issued a no-contact order, barring him from seeing Erica (and therefore Sophia) at all. Eventually, however, that order was lifted, and Martin slowly made his way back into Sophia's life.

After I got back into town, I was allowed to see Sophia on weekends. Now, I'm in a new relationship and we have kids of our own, but I still spend a lot of energy on Sophia. Currently I see her every other Sunday. I take every visit I can get, and I do everything I can to prove that I'm a good dad after all. *—Martin*

A *no-contact order* is a type of restraining order that may be used to legally prevent a parent from seeing their child or partner if some kind of domestic abuse has been alleged. (See Chapter Eight for more on domestic abuse and how to prevent it.) iIndividual no-contact orders involving fathers vary a lot, but they usually include an instruction that the father remain a certain distance away from his partner or kids and not contact them. In some cases, however, no-contact orders may allow for limited contact between a father and his partner or kids, normally supervised by a police officer or support worker.

»TRUE/FALSE«
A NO-CONTACT ORDER MEANS YOU WILL NEVER BE ABLE TO SEE YOUR KIDS AGAIN.

My ex was really manipulative. Because of the problems between us, we eventually had a no-contact order, which meant that we weren't supposed to see each other. But she knew that I wanted to see Britney no matter what, and so she'd call me and say, "You know what? C'mon over and see your daughter." Then when I did, she'd call the cops and I'd get charged with breach of probation. — *Matt*

Another reason some young fathers are absent from their kids' lives is because they doubt their sexual partners' claims that they are the children's father—or don't even know their kids exist. But missing out on a few months (or even years) doesn't have to mean missing out forever.

Aiden's mom had told me she was pregnant, but I didn't believe he was mine for a long time. It was a one-time thing between us, basically. I finally met him when he was already a few years old. I was very nervous. I didn't know what to say to him. But I remember looking into his eyes and seeing my twin. He looked just like me! —*Daniel*

By the time Daniel met Aiden, he was in a new relationship and his girlfriend Laura was pregnant with Daniel's second son, Brian. Daniel missed Aiden's first steps and first words, but he still has a chance to be Aiden's father—and he's taking it.

After Brian was born I started visiting Aiden every two weeks or so, and now I see him even more. When we're apart we use FaceTime to stay in touch. Thank God for technology! Laura loves Aiden too, which makes me really happy. She talks about him a lot and often says, "I miss Aiden!" —*Daniel*

For some young dads, even the best of intentions can go wrong. Dylan did everything he could to be a good dad to his daughter, Claire, but without her mother on board, it took a lot of persuading for child protection officials to believe he was up to the task.

> About a month and a half after Claire was born she was apprehended by child protection services. The main reason was that she was losing a lot of weight. It turned out that had to do with the fact that she was lactose intolerant, but it didn't help that we were in our teens and Samantha (Claire's mom) was caught smoking pot in the house a couple of times. Basically it didn't look good. *— Dylan*

After Claire was removed from Dylan and Samantha's custody, the couple began working to get her back. They met regularly with child protection officials and had periodic visits with Claire at her foster home. Eventually it became clear to everyone that being a parent mattered a lot more to Dylan than it did to Samantha.

»TRUE/FALSE«
CHILD PROTECTION WORKERS HAVE THE LEGAL RIGHT TO TAKE YOUR CHILDREN AWAY FROM YOU. THIS DOES NOT MEAN YOU WON'T GET THEM BACK.

> During one visit Claire peed on Samantha, and she immediately dropped everything and went to wash herself off. She got so angry that the Children's Aid official had to ask her to leave.

After that we started having separate visits with Claire, and they began noticing that I was on one end of the spectrum and Samantha was on the other. – *Dylan*

Child protection workers have the legal authority to remove children from homes where they may face a risk of harm or have been exposed to harm. The Children's Aid Society and other child protection organizations provide care to tens of thousands of children every year. Their services have also been criticized, however, for removing children from their homes too hastily—and for targeting racial-minority families and poor families that cannot afford legal representation. If you feel your family is being unfairly targeted by child protection services, get the advice of a support worker in your local community. (See the Further Resources section for more on how to access these resources.)

If you're a young dad who is separated from your child for whatever reason, know that it's never too late to reach out. Just ask Chris. He and his partner released their twins for adoption when they were in their teens. Years later he's taken a leap of faith, writing them a letter in hopes of reconnecting.

I said, "I want you to know that nobody gave you away or abandoned you. We chose parents for you who would be able to give you better lives than we could. I'd love to meet you sometime." It's in their hands now. —Chris (interviewed by CBC Radio's Aziza Sindhu in *The Boy with the Past*)

Remember: being worried your relationship won't be perfect is no reason not to have one at all. Research shows that kids generally benefit from contact with their biological dads even if it's limited or otherwise imperfect. Even if your kid doesn't respond to your attempts to initiate some kind of relationship, they will be better off knowing you want one.

You don't always have to impress your kids by taking them to Disneyland or whatever. Kids can have the time of their lives just hanging out with you at home. I think all that really matters is that you're there for your kids ... even if you're not always the perfect parent. I'm constantly second-guessing my decisions, wishing I had more money, more time, more sleep. But ultimately, I know I'm on the right track because at least I'm here, trying. —Steve

Chapter Five

RELATIONSHIPS

How becoming young parents can affect young relationships

O
nly about 20 percent of teenage parents end up getting married. And more than half don't stay together
at all. There's simply no right or wrong answer when it
comes to staying in a young relationship affected by pregnancy.
It's all about what's right for you and your partner. On the
one hand, early marriages are statistically some of the most
unstable. Studies show that couples that get married in their
teens are twice as likely to get divorced. And less than a third
of teens who marry after an unplanned pregnancy remain in
those marriages. On the other hand, teenage parents who do
stay together—married or otherwise—can sometimes have a
better quality of life, at least in the short term. In particular,
they tend to benefit financially by sharing expenses and access
to social services.

Of course, some unplanned pregnancies are the result of
sexual encounters that happen outside of relationships, but if
you are in a relationship with your sexual partner,
one thing is for sure: becoming parents should not
necessarily mean staying in a relationship. Often,
calling it quits is the right thing to do and will be
the best possible outcome for your baby as well
as for you and your partner. A decision to stay

together should be motivated by much more than a pregnancy. It should be motivated by love, respect, and a commitment to shared decision-making.

Sometimes young parents struggle to maintain a relationship because of their differing attitudes toward parenting itself. Stereotypes suggest that it's young men who are most likely to resent parenting and that young men are less inclined to play a role in their children's lives. But according to some of the fathers I spoke with, the opposite can be true too.

> Evelyn and I would both go on Facebook and see pictures of the parties we missed. And sometimes I would find myself thinking: *Well, that would have been fun.* But Evelyn was different. She would think: *God, I regret this.* In the end, motherhood at a young age became too much for her to handle. I mean, I would have moments of regret here and there, but she was totally filled with it. —*Steve*

✹✹✹

> My parents definitely didn't have the best relationship, partly because they were both so young. My dad was the responsible parent, and my mom was the fun one. She didn't care as much about the rules, which was pretty attractive to us as kids. That made my father angry. He resented always having to be the responsible parent at such a young age. —*Ethan*

***

After Samantha and I started having separate visits with Claire, the Children's Aid workers quickly realized that I was the better parent. When we were together I was able to give Samantha hints, like nudge her to get a bottle or change Claire's diaper. But without me, she didn't know when or how to do any of those things. Eventually my lawyer sat me down and said, "I have an ultimatum for you: Your wife or your daughter—pick one." It was easy: I chose Claire. —*Dylan*

Breakups are never easy. Being dumped sucks. And sometimes dumping someone else is even worse. Breaking up with a partner who became pregnant—whether you decided to parent your baby or opted for adoption or abortion—can make all the feelings ordinarily associated with a breakup that much more painful. Even if the decision to end a relationship is

mutual, feelings are probably going to be hurt. Jealousy, anger, sadness, regret, and low self-esteem are all normal emotional responses to a breakup.

Another perfectly normal part of breaking up is doubt: doubt that you're making the right decision and doubt that you and your partner will be better off apart. That sense of doubt led a number of the dads I spoke with to second-guess the wisdom of parting ways with their partners. In many cases, these young parents' relationships were on again/off again—and took a long time to end once and for all.

> Ultimately, I will always love Alisha. But I've talked to a lot of close friends who have told me—time and time again—that she is just not a good fit for me and my character. She is very closed off from expression and emotion. I think that is what allowed her to cheat on me. The first time I said, "We can make this work." She said, "I'm sorry." Then it happened again.
> —*Shane*

Everyone's approach to initiating a breakup—or dealing with one—is different. Some people decide by themselves that a relationship is over and break the news to their partner abruptly, with no negotiation. Others do everything they can to avoid having "the talk," delaying the breakup or trying to soften the blow by claiming it may not be permanent even when it is.

> She cheated on me three times. The first two times I took her back. I thought it was the right thing to do, and I wanted to make it work. But by the third time, I was like, "Okay clearly you don't want this to work." We called it a "trial" separation, but we both knew it wasn't really a trial. —*Steve*

The best approach to breaking up usually lies somewhere in between the abrupt and the prolonged. It may be unfair to break up with someone who has no idea your relationship is even in trouble! But it's also unfair to hold on to someone if either one of you knows it's not ultimately going to work out. If you're the one ending things, be honest but gentle. If you're being broken up with, ask yourself whether ending your relationship might have its advantages.

After Erica and I finally broke up I began to realize that our relationship had really poisoned me emotionally. I felt I couldn't trust anyone because of all the shit Erica had put me through. If anyone in their teens is becoming a dad— whether he planned it or not—I'd tell him to take a hard look around and ask himself if the person he's having this baby with is the right person for him. If the answer is no, don't stay in a relationship that's wrong for you. In the end, staying will only hurt your kid and you.
— *Martin*

***

A few years after the adoption, Maria and I ended up breaking up. We didn't choose an adoption because we assumed we'd break up or anything. Our relationship just sort of naturally ran its course after we had Thomas. — *Jason*

Despite all these breakup stories many young relationships do last. With the right ingredients—respect, equality, trust, communication, and hard work—there's always a chance you can build a partnership that's loving, lasting, and fulfilling.

From the moment she came out from the operation, our love has grown stronger, and we are happier, stronger people for the hardships we have faced together. She knew before the abortion that I was her lover, her protector, and her partner in life. But afterward she knew without a sliver of doubt that I would always be at her side. We became so much closer, sharing in that moment of vulnerability. — *Jackson*

***

For a number of months after our second son
Andrew was born, Catherine and I didn't see
much of each other. I would spend days at a
time sitting around feeling depressed and sorry
for myself. It wasn't until Catherine became
pregnant for a third time that I snapped out
of it. Only it turned out that this child wasn't
biologically mine—Catherine had slept with
someone else. Still, I went with her to her first
ultrasound, and I remember looking at that
screen and deciding that I would be this baby's
father. After that, things became much better
between us. – *Patrick*

Ultrasounds use sound waves to form an on-screen
picture of what's happening inside the uterus.
Doctors rely on them to monitor the development
of the fetus, determine the sex of the baby, and
check for possible complications in pregnancy.

Even the most successful relationships, built
on the most solid foundations, have their
ups and downs. Every couple will have good
days and bad days. Some good days don't
necessarily mean that a relationship is fun-
damentally a good one, but some bad days
don't mean your relationship is doomed to
fail, either.

A few months after our son Brian was born, police removed me from our house because of my drinking and some criminal charges from my past. It took a long time, and at one point I was told that I'd never be able to live with Brian and Laura (his mom) again. But eventually I checked myself into a treatment center, and I've been sober ever since. Finally, nearly three years after I first got kicked out, I'm living with my family again. —*Daniel*

Emily and I have had so many ups and downs in our relationship. She's bisexual and once cheated on me with another girl. Before we found out she was pregnant, we had already broken up and gotten back together a couple of times. And at one point I was flirting with

other girls over the Internet. But recently we've
said, "Okay. We're going to do whatever it takes
to keep this family together." I'm trying hard,
and I think she is too. At this point I feel pretty
confident that we're in it for the long haul.
— *Graeme*

After everything we've been through, Catherine
and I are really careful to take things day by day.
That's our approach. Obviously we were really
young at first and rushed right into it. And then
living apart was a huge struggle for us. We just
didn't have time to build the trust a relationship
needs to succeed. So now we're taking it slow.
— *Patrick*

Ultimately, the uncertainty of young relationships may be
another good reason to take precautions to avoid early parenthood, if you can. It certainly isn't the only way, but parenting
can be a whole lot easier with a partner. As Kale put it:

At the end of the day, I think most guys should
do their best to avoid parenthood until they
know they're really ready. How do you know?
I think mostly it has to do with meeting the
right woman. Parenting takes two. I do it alone,
but it would be a hell of a lot easier if I didn't
have to. — *Kale*

Chapter Six

ABORTION

True stories and facts about abortion from young men's point of view

Abortion is a hugely controversial topic. That's probably why this chapter was one of the most difficult to write. For starters, finding young men willing to talk about their experiences of abortion wasn't easy. After all, young women who decide to terminate their pregnancies are sometimes called irresponsible, selfish, and even sinful and young dads can experience this stigma too. Some pro-life advocates go so far as to call abortion murder.

> When my girlfriend got an abortion, the problem wasn't our families' misgivings or our own, it was the protesters. The clinic we went to was surrounded by people who badgered and shamed every woman who walked in. It hurt so much to see someone I love subjected to that. Those people were terrorizing and shaming women who were already in a scary and uncomfortable situation.
> —*Jackson*

This book is not here to take sides in the abortion debate. Decisions to terminate unplanned pregnancies happen for all kinds of reasons. For many, abortion proves to be the right decision, one they are glad they made. Sometimes, however, abortion becomes something that people regret and wish they could take back. Men whose partners decide to have abortions will inevitably have their own emotional responses, and will be affected by those of their partners. Hearing from other young men who have some experience of abortion may help.

> A *miscarriage* (the naturally occurring death of a fetus *in utero*, or in the uterus) is sometimes called a "spontaneous abortion." This is different from an "induced abortion," which is intentional and performed by a medical professional.

Part of what makes abortion such a divisive issue is that there's so much conflicting information out there. For instance, some anti-abortion activists will tell you that abortion can increase a woman's risk of breast cancer—despite the fact that it does no such thing.

When it comes to abortion, sometimes it's hard to know what to believe, and it seems like everybody has their agenda. — *Geoff*

»TRUE/FALSE«

PERFORMED BY A MEDICAL PROFESSIONAL, ABORTIONS ARE SAFE AND DO NOT INCREASE A WOMAN'S RISK OF BREAST CANCER OR OTHER DISEASE.

And while some pro-choice advocates *may* argue that there's no risk of psychological turmoil after an abortion, one of the dads I spoke to disagrees.

> I don't know why, but it just hit me one day like five or six years after the abortion. I just couldn't stop thinking about it all of the sudden. I wanted to read up on it and learn more about it. I thought it would make me feel better somehow, but it just made me feel worse. I had sort of bought into the misconception that a fetus is just a random jumble of cells, but I started learning how early organs start to form and that everything kind of develops at the same time, like a little, tiny person from really early on. That was really hard for me. —Geoff

Amidst all the conflicting information about abortion, one thing is clear: performed in proper conditions by a trained medical professional, abortion is *very safe*. In fact, the numbers show that for many moms abortion is actually safer than childbirth.

Neither of us has regrets over my girlfriend's abortion. I was twenty-two at the time, and she was twenty-four. We weren't ready, and our families have histories of depression and addiction. In our case the pregnancy also endangered her health, so to me there was no other choice. Her safety and well-being were paramount.
— *Jackson*

In most of the developed world, abortions are legal, with certain restrictions. In parts of the United States, for instance, abortions beyond the twentieth week of pregnancy are banned by law. And even in places where abortions are legal beyond week 20, access to doctors willing to perform the procedure can be hard to find. What's more, some states force women seeking an abortion to undergo counseling beforehand, which is sometimes designed to discourage them from terminating their pregnancies or make them feel guilty about doing so.

A woman's decision about whether or not to have an abortion is hers alone. After all, it's her body and her pregnancy. Some couples may benefit from having conversations about this serious decision

 and may find it helpful in making the right choice. It is your responsibility to play a supportive role no matter what the decision turns out to be.

I think that the mom should have more of a say than the dad, but not as much as she normally does. Maybe something like 60/40 when right now it's 90/10. I think that young dads make the mistake of saying, "Whatever you want ..." but they should be thinking about what they want too. — *Geoff*

I think it's wrong that men aren't usually given a choice when it comes to abortion. In every relationship I've been in, I've wanted there to be an understanding that in the event of an unplanned pregnancy, I would want to keep the baby, even if it meant becoming a single dad. — *Ethan*

For these reasons and more, it *is* important that young moms be supported in making their own decisions about abortion free from interference or coercion. But that doesn't mean young dads won't have opinions too, and they should be able to express them. That's why it's so important for young men whose partners inform them of an unplanned pregnancy to have honest and respectful conversations about abortion.

Wondering how to talk about abortion? Here are a few tips.

START EARLY. You don't necessarily need to wait until you find out about an unplanned pregnancy to start having conversations about how you might deal with one. If you feel comfortable doing so, carefully ask your partner about her thoughts on abortion after you first start having sex. Don't pick a fight, but get some idea of where you each stand.

BE HONEST. If you are against abortion, say so. If you think it would be best, say so. Be honest with your partner if you're feeling guilty or apprehensive. Likewise, expect her to be honest with you. Don't be alarmed if your partner has opinions or emotions that don't align with your own. You owe it to each other to tell the truth, even if you're not on the same page.

ASK QUESTIONS. No one expects you to know all about abortion. See the Further Resources section for a list of resources on abortion and organizations you and your partner can call with any questions you might have. You're making a big decision, and it should be an *informed* decision.

SLEEP ON IT. Yes, pregnancy demands that you make huge decisions very quickly. But you and your partner probably don't need to decide anything the *day* you find out you're expecting.

Unless she's already approaching the ninth week of her pregnancy, you'll have some time. You may immediately feel like a particular course of action is best, and it's important to trust your partner and her decision. But you should also feel free to take a day or two to think things over.

FORGIVE EACH OTHER. Ultimately you may not agree. And ultimately it's her pregnancy and her decision. But if she decides something different from what you had hoped, do what you can to forgive her.

When we found out Emily was pregnant, we went to talk to the guidance counselor at our school. She had us sit down and write out a list of pros and cons for each of our three options: abortion, adoption, and keeping the baby. For abortion, the pros were obvious: we could finish school, do the things we wanted, hang out with whoever we wanted, live our lives! The cons were pretty huge too though: the guilt, mostly. In the end, we decided together that being a family was the thing that mattered most to us.
—*Graeme*

Not long after Alisha found out she was pregnant, she brought up abortion. I knew where I stood on it: I wanted to care for the life I had brought in. Fortunately for me, she had some of her own moral conflicts around terminating the pregnancy. But ultimately we made that decision together. If she had decided otherwise, I would have had to respect that.
—*Shane*

No matter how much or how little say a young dad gets in his partner's decision about whether or not to have an abortion, her choice is sure to have an effect on him. Even if you both agree that abortion is the right decision, be sure to talk about why you feel that way and how you plan to deal with any negative emotions either of you might experience.

> We agreed right away that abortion made the most sense. But I honestly don't remember what we discussed. I think that's a sign of how little we discussed it, really. It was just something that we both kind of assumed would happen. Apart from that, I only told my parents. They weren't happy about it, of course, but they didn't seem that upset either. Honestly they gave me next to no input. — *Geoff*

Fortunately, there's a growing amount of support and information available to young women who have abortions. Unfortunately, there aren't many resources for dads. If you and your partner are considering an abortion, you may find that any medical professionals you visit focus on her and pay little attention to you. To some extent, this is understandable. She is the one undergoing the procedure not you. It may mean, however, that you have to go elsewhere to find information on what's involved in an abortion from the dad's perspective, and how your own emotional health may be affected.

No one told me how it would work. No one talked to me about what it would mean medically for my girlfriend or for the baby. I didn't even think about how it would happen, really. It was all strangely businesslike. Absolutely no resources were available to me as a dad. It felt like more of a business decision or a transaction. I wasn't present for the actual procedure, and so nobody spoke to me about how I might feel afterward. — *Geoff*

There are two main types of induced abortions: chemical and surgical. *Chemical abortions* are generally performed up to week 9 of a pregnancy. The pregnant woman takes a pill (most commonly the drug Mifepristone) that causes her body to stop producing progesterone, a hormone necessary for pregnancy to continue. *Surgical abortions* are sometimes called in-clinic abortions. They can be carried out in two ways: aspiration and D&E (dilation and evacuation). Aspiration abortion involves removing the contents of the uterus through a vacuum pump. D&E is used later on in the pregnancy and involves manually removing some tissue as well as using a vacuum pump. With both procedures, it's very important that the fetus be completely removed from the uterus, or an infection can develop. Both chemical and surgical abortions take less than 20 minutes and are very safe. Your partner may, however, experience some physical discomfort and cramping during and after the abortion.

When my girlfriend finally came out, she broke down in tears and hugged me tightly. I am a man so I have no idea, but apparently it is invasive and very uncomfortable. The only thing she said to me was "God I hope those protesters aren't still out there." — *Jackson*

It's important to take care of your partner during her abortion, and be attentive to her needs. If she asks for space, give it to her. If she asks for support, be there. But be sure to take care of yourself too. One way or another, the partners of young women who decide to terminate their pregnancies will almost certainly experience some kind of an emotional response themselves. If your experience is negative, you're not alone. And although people may try to tell you otherwise, you have every right to grieve. In fact, there are a growing number of support groups out there for dads—young and old—going through this very process. (See the Further Resources section.)

I don't think it's ever black and white. I mean, I know being a young parent can be really hard, but for me, abortion has been very hard to deal with. I know that now. — *Geoff*

If your abortion experience is positive, that's okay too. Going through with one does not make you or your partner a bad person, and neither of you should feel guilty about this choice. Each year, an estimated 44 million abortions are performed around the world. And there are as many reasons for choosing abortion as there are people involved in making those choices.

To anyone out there who is pro-life — and I mean this sincerely — good for you. Stand by your opinions. But no human being deserves to suffer through sorrow and humiliation on the level my girlfriend experienced. The people you are judging are people you don't know, and you haven't heard their stories. — *Jackson*

What matters most is respecting and supporting your partner's choice, and making sure you get reliable information about abortion from a medical professional.

I would say to any couple considering or struggling with the decision about whether or not to get an abortion: talk to each other. Open every channel of communication you can. Be honest and up front; otherwise you may resent each other afterwards. Love and support should determine what you choose, not anger or fear.
— *Jackson*

Chapter Seven

ADOPTION

Birth fathers talk about choosing adoption, and we get some advice on adoption from an expert

Fifty years ago, a vast majority of of unmarried teenagers who found themselves pregnant opted to release their children for adoption. Today that number is a lot lower, with adoptions accounting for only about 2.5 percent of teenage pregnancies. That decrease is partly thanks to reduced social stigma around being a young parent. Although young moms and dads are still subjected to all kinds of stereotyping and judgment, having a kid in your teens isn't nearly the taboo it once was. The same is true of abortion, which was a lot more difficult to access back in the 1950s. And today, we see fewer and fewer adoptions happening.

ASK AN EXPERT: Why is adoption so much less common than it once was?
Back in the fifties and sixties, society in general (and parents in particular) greatly disapproved of the whole idea of unmarried mothers and conception outside of wedlock. Fortunately, young parents today face less of this stigma and there are more supports available to them. – Dr. Gary Clapton, School of Social Work at the University of Edinburgh

Despite the huge decrease in adoption rates among teenage parents, thousands of adoptions continue to take place every year. These are different from adoptions involving kids who are in the child welfare system (i.e., foster care). Private adoption is the legal transfer of parental rights and obligations from birthparent(s) to adoptive parent(s). But that's a deceptively simple definition for a complicated and misunderstood process.

We just weren't in a place where we could take good care of a child and give them the life they'd deserve. So I brought up adoption. But at the time, we had no idea what an open adoption was or that it even existed! —*Jason*

My mom raised the question of abortion. My girlfriend and her parents said no. But everybody in the room felt that we were too young to be parents. I mean, wrapped up for my mom in it too was that if my girlfriend *didn't* have an abortion and carried the baby to term, other people would know. And it was an embarrassing thing. —*Chris* (interviewed by CBC Radio's Aziza Sindhu in *The Boy with the Past*)

There are two main types of private adoptions: closed adoptions and open adoptions. **Closed adoptions** usually involve giving up all contact with your child. Birth parents who choose closed adoptions will not be permitted to contact their children or even know about their whereabouts and well-being. Likewise, adopted children will not be able to contact their birthparents or know their identities. Some birth parents find this easier than receiving reminders of the child they gave up. But choosing closed adoption is more or less a permanent decision, and your ability to have any future contact with your child will be severely limited.

»TRUE/FALSE«

IN RARE CASES, BIRTH PARENTS WHO CHOOSE CLOSED ADOPTION MAY FIND THEIR CHILDREN LATER IN LIFE THROUGH USING AN ADOPTION REUNION REGISTRY, BUT THIS NORMALLY REQUIRES BOTH BIRTH PARENTS AND CHILDREN TO INDEPENDENTLY DECIDE TO TRY TO REUNITE.

After our twins were born, I remember I felt really proud. I wanted to go up onto the roof of the hospital and say, "I did this!" Going from feeling proud to knowing that I would probably never see them again or not see them for a long, long time ... that made me feel sad. —*Chris* (interviewed by CBC Radio's Aziza Sindhu in *The Boy with the Past*)

Open adoptions, on the other hand, involve continued contact between birth parents and adoptive parents. In most open adoptions, the child knows they are adopted and knows their birth parents. Open adoptions involve a lot more negotiation, and each arrangement is unique. In some cases, birth parents have very little contact with their children but receive periodic updates on how they're doing. In others, birth parents see their children regularly and even spend time alone with them.

> **ASK AN EXPERT: What are the pros and cons of open versus closed adoption?**
> A major pro associated with open adoption is the possibility of a continued connection with your child. That's not to say that contact will necessarily be frequent. And having to negotiate with adoptive parents may also be considered a con. Closed adoptions offer little if any possibility for future contact with the adopted child, however. In my experience, nobody "just gets on" with their life after a closed adoption or gets over the never-far emotion of wondering how their child is faring. —Dr. Gary Clapton

> I didn't see them walk. I didn't see them talk or roll over. I had wondered if once I had kids of my own some of the feeling of loss would go away because I would have something new to fill it in. It didn't. —*Chris* (interviewed by CBC Radio's Aziza Sindhu in *The Boy with the Past*)

❋❋❋

At first we weren't sure if we'd want to maintain contact with our baby. We thought it might to too hard to be reminded of what we'd given up, you know? There's part of you that would rather deal with it and move on. — *Jason*

If you and your partner decide you want to put your baby up for adoption, a registered adoption counselor can help you choose the type of adoption that's right for you. As with most parenting dilemmas, there's no right or wrong answer. Open adoption ended up being a mostly positive experience for Jason and his girlfriend Maria, but it can also be very painful to receive periodic reminders of the child you gave up. Either way, most private adoptions today allow birth parents to have some say in determining where their children end up.

The agency gave us a bunch of binders full of profiles of different parents who were looking to adopt. They had their stories and pictures and everything. And so Maria and I took those binders and began looking. I think I was looking for someone who reminded me of my own parents: driven and successful, but also down-to-earth and not too focused on work. When we came across Cyndi and Norm, they seemed perfect. — *Jason*

***

This one profile stood out because they sounded like us, ten years down the road. The husband in particular—his personality and the things that motivated him felt a lot like the things that motivated me and my personality. I saw myself in him, and we saw ourselves in them. —*Chris* (interviewed by CBC Radio's Aziza Sindhu in *The Boy with the Past*)

In most countries adoption is carefully regulated, and would-be adoptive parents must pass a home study conducted by a certified social worker. Most jurisdictions also require prospective adopters to go through some type of training before they are permitted to bring a child into their home. At least on paper, adoptive parents are some of the most prepared and qualified parents out there! Adopting from a private agency can also cost many thousands of dollars, so chances are your baby's adoptive parents will be in a good financial position to support their upbringing.

We love being able to look at where Thomas is now. It's such a great place. Every few months Cyndi and Norm will send a new e-mail with more photos. In the summer they send pictures from their cottage, and they've gone on a couple of vacations. It's cool to see him having these experiences we wouldn't have been able to give him. —*Jason*

Knowing that your kids are in a good place doesn't mean things won't be hard, however. Surrendering custody of a child is rarely an easy thing to do.

> Thomas was actually born on my twentieth birthday. Maria was exhausted afterward, and so I spent a few hours walking around the halls of the hospital singing Tom songs. The next day Cyndi and Norm came to the hospital to pick him up. We said our goodbyes, and then he went home with them. Leaving the hospital without our son was very, very hard. — *Jason*

> My girlfriend and I went with the social worker to sign the adoption papers, and then the adoptive parents were notified that they'd been born and we ... we left them there. — *Chris* (interviewed by CBC Radio's Aziza Sindhu in *The Boy with the Past*)

Whereas moms and dads who decide to parent their children tend to share their birth stories happily, people who decide on adoption or abortion are often discouraged from talking about their experiences. Research shows, however, that try as they might to "start over" after the adoption, birth parents do not simply forget that they have a child.

There's a picture of me and my girlfriend, and me holding the babies. She was fifteen and I was sixteen in this picture. It's visual evidence that it happened. I was there, and it's not just something I remember happening. —*Chris* (interviewed by CBC Radio's Aziza Sindhu in *The Boy with the Past*)

ASK AN EXPERT: How can young birth fathers expect to be affected by the experience of putting their babies up for adoption?
Birth fathers are likely to be affected in a variety of ways ranging from emotional to circumstantial. We know, for instance, that young men who gave their kids up for adoption are statistically more prone to depression, "hyper-parenting" of subsequent later children, and rocky marital/emotional relations with their partners. As well, birth fathers who part ways with the mothers of their adopted children sometimes feel a double sense of being an abandoner—both of their baby and its mom. If you're a young birth father plagued by any of these negative emotions, know that what you're experiencing is normal, and take care of yourself: meet up with other birth fathers who have given up their kids. Share your story with them or with someone else you trust. —Dr. Gary Clapton

It's like there was a piece of me that was missing and out there somewhere, and I had no idea where. I wondered whenever I saw kids with their parents that seemed like they were siblings and maybe twins if that might be them. I searched a lot of faces ... babies and kids to see if any looked at all familiar or anything like me or like her. — *Chris* (interviewed by CBC Radio's Aziza Sindhu in *The Boy with the Past*)

If you and your partner are considering adoption, it's very important to seek the advice of a professional familiar with adoption laws in your area. The exact ways in which adoption works can vary from one location to the next, but services for birth parents thinking about adoption are usually free. (See the Further Resources section for a list of resources to help you find location-specific information on open and closed adoptions in your state/province.) As Chris and Jason both acknowledge, adoption is far from easy, but it may ultimately be the right decision for you and your partner.

A lot of people think about adoption as a last resort or a negative thing, but for us it was a really good experience. It's cool to see how happy Thomas and his adoptive parents are and to know that they really deserve that. Obviously this wasn't planned for me. I mean, we were using protection when Maria got pregnant. It was a total accident, but I don't think of it as a shitty situation anymore. I think of it as a blessing. — *Jason*

Chapter Eight

COPING WITH STRESS

Young fathers talk about the stress associated with parenthood and where they found support

> Every Monday I play floor hockey with a group of other young dads. It's honestly so great to hang out with them and get a bit of my aggression out through sport. I met one of my best friends at those hockey games, and I was actually best man in his wedding last year. It really helps to make those connections and find people in the same situation to talk to. It makes you feel like you're not alone. —*Matt*

Being a young parent can be an extremely isolating experience. Many young dads decide to drop out of full-time school, meaning they see less of their friends and classmates. And young dads who have already graduated will often find it harder to stay in touch with other people their age. If your partner decides to get an abortion, or you and your partner release your child for adoption, you may have a hard time interacting with people who have no way of knowing what you've experienced.

When you're a teenage parent you can't really
turn to your friends. None of them has kids.
None of them really understands what you're
going through. —*Shane*

It's never an easy thing to say to someone.
There's no casual way to be like, "So ... I have
a kid." Usually whoever I'm talking to is like:
"Whoa! Really?! Are you serious?" —*Jason*

Chapter Five is a reminder that early parenthood can also
put a strain on your relationship with your baby's mom—the
one person who knows what you're going through! And many
young parents find that their relationships with their *own*
moms and dads suffer. Even if they're supportive, your parents may disapprove of your relationship, your decisions about
how to deal with a pregnancy, or the fact that you got a young
woman pregnant in the first place. Odds are this will leave you
feeling pretty alone at times.

The stress and isolation associated with parenthood can
sometimes contribute to an increased risk of domestic
abuse in the homes of young moms and dads. Sadly,
research confirms that child abuse is more common
among adolescent parents. And young fathers are also
more likely to come from abusive homes themselves.
These factors—combined with money troubles, relationship problems, and sleeplessness—can make it
easy to lose your temper and lash out.

Don't lose your temper. I know I've lost my
temper a couple of times in front of Ashley, and
she's been scared by it. That's a terrible feeling.
It brings you back down pretty fast when you
see your kid look at you with scared eyes.
Blowing up makes you say hurtful things you
shouldn't have, things that will come back to
kick you in the butt later. Do whatever it takes
not to bottle up until you blow up. — *Matt*

Coping with stress is therefore hugely important not only for
your own well-being but also for the safety of those around
you. Today there are many supports available to victims of
domestic abuse—as there should be! There are also some
resources and programs available to men who think they may
be abusers. The trouble is, it can be really difficult to recognize
whether you are behaving in a way that could be physically
or mentally harmful to your partner or child. The National
Domestic Violence Hotline in the United States suggests you
start by asking yourself some of the following questions:

Do you
- get angry when your partner or child doesn't act the way
  you want?
- blame your anger on drugs, alcohol, or your family's
  actions?
- find it very difficult to control your anger and
  calm down?
- express your anger by threatening to hurt your
  partner/child or actually physically doing so?

- express your anger verbally through raising your voice, calling your partner/child names, or using put-downs?
- get angry or insecure about your partner's relationships with others?
- frequently call and text to check up on your partner, or have them check in with you?
- feel like your partner needs to ask your permission to go out, get a job, go to school, or spend time with others?

Sometimes it can be easy to dismiss these kinds of behaviors as being "out of character" or a way of "letting off steam." In reality, these are all warning signs of abuse and should be taken very seriously. (See the Further Resources section for a list of resources—including anonymous 24-hour hotlines— that deal with domestic abuse.)

> The US Department of Justice defines *domestic violence* as "a pattern of abusive behavior in any relationship that is used by one partner to gain or maintain power and control over another intimate partner. Domestic violence can be physical, sexual, emotional, economic, or psychological actions or threats of actions that influence another person."

»TRUE/FALSE«

SOME WOMEN ARE ABUSERS, BUT A VAST MAJORITY OF PEOPLE COMMITTING DOMESTIC VIOLENCE ARE MEN.

While there's no excuse for abuse, change is possible, and it starts with taking responsibility for your actions. It also starts with reaching out for help when you need it. Remember: excessive stress and low self-esteem can contribute hugely to the risk of abuse. So alleviating your stress is crucial. For many of the dads I spoke with, that meant finding other young fathers to talk to.

> I would definitely tell other young dads to take some parenting courses. I've done a lot of them—probably about five or six altogether. Listening to other parents that are going through the same stuff as you is really helpful. You're able to insert your own ideas and grab some knowledge off other young parents. It can be hard to admit that there are things you've got to learn, but it helped me a lot once I did. —*Daniel*

Stress is a normal part of life, but for some young dads the stress that is *ordinarily* associated with parenting gives rise to more extreme emotions associated with anxiety and depression. As discussed in Chapter One, it's important to learn how to tell the difference between normal levels of stress and unhealthy levels. Often that difference is the degree to which your stress interferes with your ability to perform day-to-day tasks and live a normal life. If you're finding it difficult to get out of bed in the morning, get to work, or enjoy time with friends and family, it's time to get help.

> If you ever feel like you might want to hurt yourself or end your life, call 911 or a suicide hotline right away. You can also check out the Further Resources section for a list of mental health resources.

After Shane and his girlfriend Alisha broke up, he became a single dad to their two kids, Michael and Angela. With the help of a local support center for young parents he was able to manage at first. Support workers set Shane and the kids up with an apartment and gave them a monthly allowance. They helped Shane with budgeting and taught him about infant nutrition and meal planning. But after a year of successful single parenting, the stress started to catch up with Shane again.

> Despite the great support I was getting, single fatherhood was becoming too much for me to handle. I was gaining a lot of weight. I was irritable all the time. Finally one of my social workers sat me down and said, "Shane, can you be the father that Michael and Angela need right now?" and I was forced to admit that the answer was no. I cried then. I cried so hard.
> — *Shane*

After admitting he needed help, Shane contacted his kids' mom and asked her to take over childcare for a while. He temporarily surrendered primary caregiver status to her and took some time to look after himself.

> During that time, one of my social workers told me that I might be suffering from postpartum depression. I remember being like, "Really?!" I had always thought that was something that only affected women. But they explained that it's actually not uncommon for men to experience it and that I was displaying a lot of the symptoms. After that I was able to start working on a lot of my insecurities, and my confidence improved a lot. —*Shane*

Postpartum depression most commonly affects women but can also affect men. It is a form of mental illness that can occur following the birth of a child. Like regular depression, postpartum is about more than the odd "bad day." It comes in the form of continual and persistent mood swings and is made worse by sleep deprivation. A new dad or mom experiencing postpartum depression may feel like a bad parent and may even have frightening thoughts about harming their baby or themselves. If this describes you or your partner seek medical help right away, and don't hesitate to call 911.

»TRUE/FALSE«
POSTPARTUM DEPRESSION AFFECTS ONLY WOMEN.

At its most basic, stress is the body's response to a dangerous situation. In prehistoric times, stress was a mechanism that helped people escape predators, for instance. That's why people sometimes talk about stress as the body's way of telling us we either have to "fight" or "take flight." The body does this by releasing a variety of hormones that speed up our heart rate and breathing, and increase our blood pressure. Over a short period of time, or in a genuinely life-threatening situation, stress can help us survive. Sustained over many weeks, months, or years, however, the presence of these stress-related hormones in the bloodstream can lead to chronic fatigue, decreased appetite, a weakened immune system, and other health issues.

After Maria and I found out she was pregnant, I spent a number of weeks traveling back and forth between school and home while we were figuring everything out with the adoption. It was really distracting and difficult. I'm still amazed that I didn't fail all my exams that year.
—*Jason*

Needless to say, stress can take a toll on our bodies at the best of times. But research also shows that young men and women are *especially* affected. This is because our brains continue developing well into our teens and even twenties. That's why teenagers and young adults are especially prone to a variety of mental illnesses. This ongoing brain development means that hormonal responses to stress are not always well regulated.

> The stress involved in raising three kids on my own has honestly been more than I thought I could bear at times. There have been some days when I've felt like I was on the verge of a mental breakdown or like I might have a heart attack. I love my kids and wouldn't give them up for the world, but there's only a certain amount of stress the human body can take. — *Steve*

Even if stress doesn't lead to symptoms as extreme as Shane's or Steve's, it deserves to be taken seriously. The good news is that there are almost as many techniques for coping with stress as there are stressed-out young dads. Nearly every one of the young dads I spoke to had developed their own.

> Fatherhood is a constant learning curve, but the best part is figuring things out. You're like a detective, almost. Kieran would be crying, whining, hungry, and I'd figure it

out. When he was really young, I made a little checklist of things that might be wrong when he was crying, and I learned which problems were most likely to occur at which times of day. I developed this trial-and-error process and kept careful notes. — *Kale*

It's good to keep busy. I find myself getting more anxious if all I'm doing is sitting around, thinking about things—that's when it can start to feel overwhelming. Whenever I think too much I get really stressed out, but if I'm active and keeping myself busy, it's a lot easier to focus on the positives. — *Patrick*

Fortunately, research shows that despite the high levels of stress associated with young parenthood, men and women who became parents at an early age are no more likely to suffer from *lasting* psychological problems than those who become parents later in life. And if the stress feels like too much to deal with in the meantime, rest assured that things will get better as your newborn gets older.

When you're dealing with a three-month-old who's not getting any sleep it can be easy to think, oh man, are the next eighteen years of my life going to be like that? They're not. I never would have wanted a second kid if Gemma hadn't grown out of that. — *Steve*

***

I definitely look forward to a day when they're a bit more grown up. I think it will be cool because when they're in their teens I'll still technically be a young dad, so we can enjoy the same things. We can play guitar together and shoot hoops, and they won't be able to say, "Dad, you're so old!" And then when they're eighteen I can ship them off and still be relatively young and enjoy some of the things I've had to give up for the time being. — *Patrick*

***

I had my first daughter when I was just twenty-two and my second much later, in my thirties. The first time I was so stressed that I ended up in hospital, but the second time I knew what to expect. I knew to sleep when she was sleeping.

> I knew she wasn't going to break if I held her.
> When she was crying, I could tell if it was an "I
> need my diaper changed" cry or a "feed me" cry.
> — *Matt*

As helpful as it can be to reach out to others for comfort and advice, it's also important to retain a sense of autonomy. You are your child's only biological father. And as *any* parent will tell you, raising kids is something almost everyone has an opinion about. Sometimes these opinions will contradict one another—or will go against your own instincts about what's right for you and your family. Ultimately the decisions you make are yours and yours alone.

A lot of people are still shocked when they find out I'm a single dad. But twenty years ago, people would have been shocked if you *didn't* have kids by the time you were twenty-five. My sister didn't get married until she was thirty, and people gave her a really hard time. So it almost seems like no matter when you have kids or get married or whatever, there will be someone who thinks it was too early … or too late.
— *Steve*

***

Everyone will have an opinion about how you
should raise your kid. Ask for help, by all means,
but at the end of the day do things your way.
There's really no wrong way to do things as
long as your kids are safe, happy, fed, and clean.
—*Matt*

FURTHER RESOURCES

Many of the resources listed below provide information related to more than one aspect of pregnancy or parenting, but they're divided into categories based on their main focus. Some of them are geared primarily toward moms, but if they're listed here they also contain information young dads may find useful.

ON PREGNANCY:

Planned Parenthood (www.plannedparenthood.org) is one of the most comprehensive websites when it comes to information on pregnancy, as well as birth control, STDs, sexual health, childbirth, relationships, and more. Be sure to explore the site and find the pages that are most relevant to you. You can also use the search function to look up specific articles.

Teen Health Source (www.teenhealthsource.com) is an excellent resource on sexual health, birth control, pregnancy, relationships, and more for youth.

The book *The Expectant Father: Facts, Tips, and Advice for Dads-to-Be* by Armin Brott and Jennifer Ash deals with some of the emotional, financial, and physical changes fathers may experience during their partners' pregnancies.

Today's Parent (www.todaysparent.com) website is mostly geared toward moms but has some useful resources for expectant fathers. Its week-by-week pregnancy guide has information on foods to avoid, sex during pregnancy, morning sickness, prenatal vitamins, and more.

ON CHILDBIRTH:

Baby Center (www.babycenter.com) has—along with many other resources—some good information on different types of childbirth classes for couples and the best ways to access them. It also gives registered users access to online childbirth classes they can take remotely and for free.

Husband and wife Elissa Stein and Jon Lichtenstein's book *Don't Just Stand There: How to Be Helpful, Clued-In, Supportive, Engaged, Meaningful, and Relevant in the Delivery Room* is a pocket-sized, illustrated guide to childbirth for dads. It's small enough to take to the hospital with you, and deals with the stages of labor, what to bring to the delivery room, and more. It also has contributions from an OB-GYN and a doula.

The book *The Birth Partner: A Complete Guide to Childbirth for Dads, Doulas, and All Other Labor Companions* by Penny Simkin is written for everyone supporting women through childbirth. It contains information on how to know when labor has begun, medications women can take to decrease their pain, natural birth techniques, and post-childbirth care.

ORGANIZATIONS OFFERING SUPPORT TO YOUNG OR FIRST-TIME DADS:

Note: The following is a somewhat random sampling of support groups and organizations. This list is far from exhaustive, but it contains links to websites that can help you find additional supports not listed here.

IN THE UNITED STATES:

Boot Camp for New Dads (www.bootcampfornewdads.org) is an initiative based in California that offers parenting classes for first-time fathers in over 200 communities across the United States. Their workshops are run by "veteran" dads and are available in virtually every state and multiple languages: 949-754-9067.

In Alabama, the **Children's Trust Fund** (http://ctf.state.al.us) runs a number of programs for young fathers that deal with parenting issues ranging from child support to general life skills: 334-242-5710.

In Maryland, the **Center for Urban Families** (CFUF) runs programs to help fathers learn how to play an active role in parenting. The Center also conducts home visits, individual counseling sessions, domestic violence workshops, and more: 410-367-5691.

In New York City, **Inwood House** (www.inwoodhouse.com) is an organization that helps meet the needs of pregnant and parenting teens, particularly low-income and racial-minority mothers and fathers: 212-861-4400.

In the Los Angeles area, **Project Fatherhood** (www.project-fatherhood.org) runs a range of different support groups for young fathers, including its flagship Men in Relationships Group and a support group designed to help out-of-work fathers find employment: 213-260-7604.

Catholic Charities USA is a group of more than 160 local Catholic agencies across the United States, many of which offer faith-based programming for young fathers and families. For example, the Brooklyn and Queens chapter (www.ccbq.org) runs the **Man Up Fatherhood Program**, which helps dads aged sixteen to twenty-four bond with their children, deal with stress, and become financially independent: 347-915-0530.

In the Camden, New Jersey, area, **Fathers on Track** is a free educational and support program that offers sessions focusing on child development, positive discipline, sexuality, teen parent relationships, and more: 856-365-3519, ext. 223.

This is just a small sample of the many programs available for young fathers across the United States. The US federal government also has a **Connect with Programs** feature (www.fatherhood.gov/for-dads/connect-with-programs) that can help dads find local supports not mentioned here.

IN CANADA:

Edmonton, **Terra Centre** (terracentre.ca) offers a number of supports for young dads, including home visits, parenting classes, and monthly group activities with other young dads: 780-428-3772.

Alberta's **Family Resource Facilitation Program** (www.frfp. ca) has information on a number of parent education programs across the province.

In Abbotsford, the **Abby Dads Father Involvement Program** (www.abbydads.ca) offers individual support for fathers (including counseling over coffee and a range of group programs for young fathers, from parenting classes to weekly floor hockey games with other young dads: 604-859-7681.

In Surrey, the organization **Young Families/Youth Unlimited** (www.youngfamilies.ca) runs a support group for young fathers called Stepping Up, which offers weekly hockey games, Dad's and Tots' Breakfasts, and one-on-one mentoring: 604-202-8914.

In Victoria, **Young Parents Support Network** (www.ypsn.ca) supports young moms and dads through parenting programs and one-on-one counseling: 250-384-0552.

In Toronto, the **Young and Potential Fathers Initiative** (www. youngpfathers.org) runs a number of support groups in partnership with the YMCA. These include a weekly discussion group with other young fathers called Fatherhood Talk, which comes with a free haircut! 416-916-2512, ext. 305.

In Toronto, **Planned Parenthood Toronto** offers the **Time Out** program for young parents and parents-to-be. This weekly drop-in group welcomes young mothers and fathers and can help connect you with the resources and tools you need to make healthy, informed decisions for yourself and your family: 416-961-0113 x154.

Ottawa's **Young Parent Support Network** (www.ottaway-oungparents.com) runs a weekly evening drop-in for young dads, as well as a ten-week parenting program just for fathers: 613-749-4584.

This is just a small sample of the many programs available for young fathers. Check out the **Canadian Association of Family Resource Programs** (www.frp.ca) for more on various local supports not mentioned here. And you can also try contacting a local YMCA, many of which run great pre- and postnatal programs for parents young and old.

ELSEWHERE:

In Australia, **Parentline** (www.parentline.com.au) is a national hotline that responds to questions about parenting for the cost of a local call: 1300 30 1300 in Queensland and the Northern Territory; 13 22 89 in Victoria; 1300 364 100 in South Australia; 1300 1300 52 in New South Wales; and 1800 654 432 in Western Australia.

In the UK, the **Young Dads Council** (YoungDadsCouncil. co.uk) is made up of dads and expectant dads age twenty-five and under. They work to improve services for young fathers.

Also in the UK, the **Dads UK Forum** (www.dads-uk.co.uk) has a variety of chat threads and links available to fathers young and old.

GENERAL RESOURCES ON PARENTING:

The **National Fatherhood Initiative** (www.fatherhood.org), a nonprofit organization based in the United States, is committed to involving fathers in parenthood. It primarily supports other agencies offering programming on fatherhood, but also has some resources for current or soon-to-be dads themselves, including an e-book on connecting with your child, and an interactive Countdown to Growing Up Tool that helps dads learn what to expect from their child's growth and development: 301-948-0599.

The website **Dads Adventure** (www.dadsadventure.com) has a unique Ask a Dad featurethat allows you to submit a question to a group of experienced fathers, as well as browse other dads' questions and answers.

The website **DIY Father** (diyfather.com) has pages devoted to each three of the first twelve months of a baby's life. It also provides information on topics ranging from the toddler years, to infant nutrition, to co-sleeping, and more.

The book *Teen Dads: Rights, Responsibilities & Joys* by Jeanne Warren Lindsay is one of few other resources targeted specifically at young fathers. Like this book you're holding, the most recent edition of *Teen Dads* includes quotes from real-life young fathers sharing their experiences.

The book *Be Prepared: A Practical Handbook for New Dads* by Gary Greenberg and Jeannie Hayden is a lighthearted look at the first year of parenting, complete with advice on how to change a baby at a packed sports stadium, how to handle sleeplessness, and more.

ON MAKING ENDS MEET:

Many of the resources listed above provide some information on finding work and budgeting, in addition to other useful parenting tips. If you're in high school or college, you will also have access to a number of supports through your school's guidance services.

The book *Will the Dollars Stretch? Teen Parents Living on Their Own* by Sudie Pollock is a collection of five short stories about teen parents striving to be financially independent. The reader writes the characters' checks and balances their checkbooks to get a feel for the real struggles of many young parents.

The **American Job Center** (www.jobcenter.usa.gov/youth) has a list of resources to help young people find work in the United States.

In Ontario, **Youth Employment Services** (www.yes.on.ca) offers résumé-writing workshops, help with job searching, and more. It has an 83 percent success rate at helping young people find work.

Elsewhere in Canada, the federal government's **Services for Youth** site (www.youth.gc.ca) provides a variety of resources on developing job skills, finding references, generating a résumé, completing a job search, and preparing for an interview.

ON FINISHING SCHOOL:

In Canada, the **Services for Youth** site (www.youth.gc.ca) has a comprehensive list of resources on finishing high school, by province.

In the United States, the American Council on Education's **GED Testing Service** (www.gedtestingservice.com) can be used by anyone in the country preparing for a GED exam.

ON DEALING WITH CHILD PROTECTION SERVICES:

Many of the agencies already mentioned here employ social workers who can help you prepare for interactions with child protection service officials.

If your child is apprehended by child protection services, you will almost certainly need legal representation to regain custody. Online services such as **FindLaw** (lawyers.findlaw.com) can help you find a lawyer in your area of the United States specializing in Father's Rights or Family Law.

In the United States and Canada, young parents looking for legal representation may be eligible for legal aid, which provides legal services to low-income individuals. Google "legal aid" and your location to find a local office. Unfortunately, most legal aid programs are underfunded, so there is usually not enough money to go around.

The **Texas Department of Family and Protective Services** (www.dfps.state.tx.us) has a good list of Frequently Asked Questions on dealing with child protection services, which dads may find useful no matter where they're located.

ON CHILD SUPPORT:

The regulations that govern child support vary from jurisdiction to jurisdiction. In Canada, guidelines can be found at the **Department of Justice** website (www.justice.gc.ca) under Family Law, Child Support.

In the United States, child support is overseen by the **Office of Child Support Enforcement** (www.acf.hhs.gov/programs/css), which has an easy-to use map that can help you find a case worker in your area to answer any questions you may have about making or receiving child support payments. The Office also publishes a free, downloadable *Child Support*

Handbook, which discusses how child support payments are calculated, made, and enforced.

ON RELATIONSHIPS:

In addition to offering general information on pregnancy and childbirth, **Planned Parenthood** (www.plannedparenthood. org/health-info/relationships) has lots of useful information on how to tell whether you're in a healthy relationship, how to make a relationship last, and how to end a relationship when it's time.

TeensHealth (teenshealth.org) is another great site with advice on how to break up, get over a breakup, and deal with abuse in relationships.

ON ABORTION:

Once again, **Planned Parenthood** (www.plannedparenthood. org/health-info/abortion) comes to the rescue with easy-to-understand information on abortion, including detailed descriptions of chemical and surgical abortion procedures, parental consent laws, and postabortion care.

If you have any questions about abortion, unplanned pregnancies, or related issues, another useful site is http://prochoice. org/think-youre-pregnant/naf-hotline/

For fathers who are struggling with feelings of guilt or regret following an abortion, **Fatherhood Forever** (www.

fatherhoodforever.org) and **Reclaiming Fatherhood** (www.
menandabortion.info). These websites and others like them
provide resources for dads struggling with postabortion grief,
testimony from other fathers, and information on accessing
support groups. Resources like these can be extremely helpful, but young dads should know that many organizations
offering postabortion support are faith-based and effectively
antiabortion.

ON ADOPTION:

The **Adoption Council of Canada** (www.adoption.ca) has a
ton of resources for everyone involved in the adoption process:
birth parents, adoptive parents, and adoptees. This includes
information on adoption law in different provinces and ter-
ritories, a list of private domestic adoption agencies across the
country, and information on reuniting with children placed in
adoptive homes.

In the United States, **adoption.com** is a similar resource offering guidance on dealing with unplanned pregnancy, browsing
adoptive parent profiles, and navigating adoption law. For registered users (it's free) there's also a forum where birth fathers
can interact with one another and share their stories.

To listen to Aziza Sindhu's documentary on birth dad Chris
Farley Ratcliffe, visit www.cbc.ca/thecurrent and search for
"The Boy with the Past."

ON DOMESTIC ABUSE:

In the United States and Canada, **The National Domestic Violence Hotline** (www.thehotline.org) provides around-the-clock information and guidance to anyone dealing with abuse in the home, whether they are the victim or the abuser. Calls to the hotline are confidential, and responders will remain supportive and empathetic no matter what your situation: 1-800-799-SAFE (7233).

In Australia, the **National Sexual Assault, Domestic Family Violence Counselling Service** (www.1800respect.org.au) provides similar services: 1800 737 732.

Elsewhere, the **HotPeachPages** website (www.hotpeachpages. net) has a comprehensive list of domestic abuse hotlines and resources all around the world.

Be sure to check out **Men Stopping Violence** (www.men-stoppingviolence.org) for more information on domestic abuse prevention and links to a number of violence prevention groups in the United States.

IN A CRISIS:

Never hesitate to call 911 in an emergency.

BIBLIOGRAPHY

INTRODUCTION

Kearney, M., & Levine, P. (2014). Media influences on social outcomes: The impact of MTV's 16 and Pregnant on teen childbearing (Working Paper No. 19795). *NBER Working Paper Series.*

Martins, N., & Clairesen, R. (2014). The relationship between "teen mom" reality programming and teenagers' beliefs about teen parenthood. *Mass Communication and Society, 17*(6), 830–852.

FINDING OUT

Barrett, G., Smith, S. C., & Wellings, K. (2004). Conceptualisation, development, and evaluation of a measure of unplanned pregnancy. *Journal of Epidemiology and Community Health, 58*(5), 426–433.

Coleman, L., & Cater, S. (2006). "Planned" teenage pregnancy: Perspectives of young women from disadvantaged backgrounds in England. *Journal of Youth Studies, 9*(5), 593–614.

Daniel, J. (2011). Contraceptive efficacy. In R. Hatcher et al. (Eds.), *Contraceptive technology* (pp. 779–863). New York: Ardent Media.

Elster, A., & Panzarine, S. (1983). Teenage fathers: Stresses during gestation and early parenthood. *Clinical Pediatrics, 22*(10), 700–703.

Fennell, J., Blanchard, K., Jones, R., & Higgins, J. (2009). Better than nothing or savvy risk-reduction practice? The importance of withdrawal. *Contraception, 79*(6), 407–410.

Finer, L. B., & Zolna, M. R. (2011). Unintended pregnancy in the United States: Incidence and disparities, 2006. *Contraception, 84*(5), 478–485.

Henshaw, S., & Finer, L. (2006). Disparities in rates of unintended pregnancy in the United States, 1994 and 2001. *Perspectives on Sexual and Reproductive Health, 38*(2), 90–96.

Martin, J., Hamilton, B., Osterman, M., Curtin, S., & Mathews, T. (2013). Births: Final data for 2012. *National Vital Statistics Reports, 62*(9): Table A. Retrieved from http://www.cdc.gov/nchs/data/nvsr/nvsr62/nvsr62_09.pdf

Montgomery, K. S. (2002). Planned adolescent pregnancy: What they wanted. *Journal of Pediatric Health Care, 16*(6), 282–289.

Mosher, W., Martinez G., Chandra A., Abma J., & Willson S. (2004). Use of contraception and use of family planning services in the United States: 1982–2002. *Advance Data No. 350.*

Planned Parenthood. (n.d.). Morning-after pill (emergency contraception). Retrieved from http://www.plannedparenthood.org/health-info/morning-after-pill-emergency-contraception

Sindhu, A. (2012, February 9). The Boy with the Past. [CBC Radio]. *The Current.* Retrieved from http://www.cbc.ca/thecurrent/episode/2012/02/09/the-boy-with-the-past-documentary/

PREGNANCY AND CHILDBIRTH

Central Intelligence Agency. (2010). Country comparison: Maternal mortality rate. In *The CIA World Factbook.* Retrieved from https://www.cia.gov/library/publications/the-world-factbook/rankorder/2223rank.html

PARENTING

General Educational Development Testing Service. (2009). *Technical manual: 2002 Series GED tests.* Retrieved from http://www.gedtestingservice.com/uploads/files/cf2fe07cf44bff4d89e01ab949d145dc.pdf

Kids Health. (2014). *Sleep and newborns.* Retrieved from http://kidshealth.org/parent/growth/sleep/sleepnewborn.html#

Liu, S., et al. (2007). Maternal mortality and severe morbidity associated with low-risk planned cesarean delivery versus planned vaginal delivery at term. *Canadian Medical Association Journal, 176*(4), 455–460.

Taheri, S., et al. (2004). Short sleep duration is associated with reduced leptin, elevated ghrelin, and increased body mass index. *PLOS Medicine, 1*(3), 210–217.

FATHER FROM AFAR

Feldstein, A. (2014, October 2). What most people don't know about "deadbeat parents" and child support. *The Huffington Post.* Retrieved from http://www.huffingtonpost.ca/andrew-feldstein/deadbeat-parents-child-support_b_5921226.html

Harper, C., & McLanahan, S. (2004). Father absence and youth incarceration. *Journal of Research on Adolescence, 14*(3), 369–397.

Howard, K., et al. (2006). Fathers' influence in the lives of children with adolescent mothers. *Journal of Family Psychology, 20*(3), 468–476.

Kreider, R., & Ellis, R. (2011, June). *Living arrangements of children: 2009.* Washington, DC: United States Census Bureau. Retrieved from http://www.census.gov/prod/2011pubs/p70-126.pdf

National Fatherhood Initiative. (2014). There is a "father factor" in our nation's worst social problems. Retrieved from http://www.fatherhood.org/father-absence-statistics

Rhein, L., et al. (1996). Teen father participation in childrearing: Family perspectives. *Journal of Adolescent Health, 18*(2), 121–121.

Robinson, B. (1988). Teenage pregnancy from the father's perspective. *American Journal of Orthopsychiatry, 58*(1), 46–51.

Schaefer, N. (2007, November 16). The corrupt business of child protective services. *From the legislative desk of Senator Nancy Schaefer 50th District of Georgia.* Retrieved from http://www.nccr.info/attachments/600_The%20Corrupt%20Business%20Of%20Child%20Protective%20Services.pdf

Teachman, J. (2004). The childhood living arrangements of children and the characteristics of their marriages. *Journal of Family Issues, 25*(1), 86–111.

RELATIONSHIPS

Berglas, N., Brindis, C., & Cohen, J. (2003, June). *Adolescent pregnancy and childbearing in California* Report CRB-03-007. Sacramento, CA: California Research Bureau. Retrieved from http://www.library.ca.gov/crb/03/07/03-007a.pdf

Gillmore, M. R., et al. (2008). Marriage following adolescent parenthood: Relationship to adult well-being. *Journal of Marriage and Family, 70,* 1136–1144.

Kershaw, S. (2008, September 3). Now, the bad news on teenage marriage. *The New York Times*, p. G1. Retrieved from http://www.nytimes.com/2008/09/04/fashion/04marriage.html

National Campaign to Prevent Teen Pregnancy. (2002, February). *Not just another single issue: Teen pregnancy prevention's link to other critical social issues.* Retrieved from http://eric.ed.gov/?id=ED462522

Seiler, N. (2002, April). *Is teen marriage a solution?* Washington, DC: Center for Law and Social Policy.

TeensHealth. (2014). How to break up respectfully. Retrieved from http://teenshealth.org/teen/your_mind/relationships/break-up.html?tracking=T_RelatedArticle#

ABORTION

Grimes, D., et al. (2006, November 25). Unsafe abortion: The preventable pandemic. *The Lancet, 368*(9550), 1908–1919.

Planned Parenthood. (n.d.) Abortion. Retrieved from http://www.plannedparenthood.org/health-info/abortion

Sedgh, G., et al. (2012). Induced abortion: Incidence and trends worldwide from 1995 to 2008. *The Lancet, 379*(9816), 625–632.

World Health Organization. (2000, June). Induced abortion does not increase breast cancer risk (Fact Sheet 240). Archived from the original on 13 February 2011. Retrieved from http://web.archive.org/web/20110104013629/http://www.who.int/mediacentre/factsheets/fs240/en/

ADOPTION

Adoption Council of Canada. (n.d.). Adoption in Canada. Retrieved from http://www.adoption.ca/adoption-in-canada

Adoption Council of Canada. (n.d.). Frequently Asked Questions about Adoption. Retrieved from http://www.adoption.ca/faqs

MacDonald, M., & McSherry, D. (2011). Open adoption: Adoptive parents' experiences of birth family contact and talking to their child about adoption. *Adoption and Fostering, 35*(3). pp. 4–16.

Planned Parenthood. (2013). *Pregnancy and childbearing among U.S. teens.* New York: Planned Parenthood Federation of America, Inc.

Resnick, M. D. (1992). Adolescent pregnancy options. *Journal of School Health, 62*(7), 298–303.

Silverman, P., et al. (1988). Reunions between adoptees and birth parents: The birth parents' experience. *Social Work. 33*(6), 523–528.

COPING WITH STRESS

Bergland, C. (2013, December 19). Why is the teen brain so vulnerable? *Psychology Today.* Retrieved from http://www.psychologytoday.com/blog/the-athletes-way/201312/why-is-the-teen-brain-so-vulnerable

Canadian Mental Health Association. (n.d.). Postpartum depression. Retrieved from http://www.cmha.ca/mental_health/postpartum-depression/#.VEVHovl4pcQt

Marshall, E., Buckner, E., & Powell, K. (2007). Evaluation of a teen parent program designed to reduce child abuse and neglect and to strengthen families. *Journal of Child and Adolescent Psychiatric Nursing, 4*(3), pp. 96–100.

She Knows. (2009, November 12). Domestic abuse: Help for the batterer. Retrieved from http://www.sheknows.com/living/articles/3884/domestic-abuse-help-for-the-batterer

Taylor, J. (2009). Midlife impacts of adolescent parenthood. *Journal of Family Issues,* 30(4), 484–510.

TeensHealth. (n.d.). What is stress? Retrieved from http://
kidshealth.org/teen/your_mind/emotions/stress.html

WebMD. (n.d.). The effects of stress on your body. Retrieved from
http://www.webmd.com/balance/stress-management/
effects-of-stress-on-your-body

Wekerle, C., & Wolfe, D. (1993). Prevention of child physical
abuse and neglect: Promising new directions. *Clinical
Psychology Review, 13,* 501–540.

TRUE/FALSE ANSWERS

Chapter One:
Page 14: False
Page 18: False
Page 22: True
Chapter Two:
Page 28: True
Chapter Three:
Page 43: False
Chapter Four:
Page 53: False
Page 55: True
Chapter Six:
Page 71: True
Chapter Seven:
Page 85: True
Chapter Eight:
Page 96: True
Page 100: False

INDEX